THE
LAST
WEEK

THE
LAST
WEEK

The Day-by-Day Account of
Jesus's Final Week in Jerusalem

MARCUS J. BORG
AND
JOHN DOMINIC CROSSAN

HarperSanFrancisco
A Division of HarperCollins*Publishers*

THE LAST WEEK: *The Day-by-Day Account of Jesus's Final Week in Jerusalem.* Copyright ©
2006 by Marcus J. Borg and John Dominic Crossan. All rights reserved. Printed in the
United States of America. No part of this book may be used or reproduced in any manner
whatsoever without written permission except in the case of brief quotations embodied in
critical articles and reviews. For information address HarperCollins Publishers, 10 East
53rd Street, New York, NY 10022.

HarperCollins books may be purchased for educational, business, or sales promotional use.
For information please write: Special Markets Department, HarperCollins Publishers, 10
East 53rd Street, New York, NY 10022.

HarperCollins Web site: http://www.harpercollins.com
HarperCollins®, ■®, and HarperSanFrancisco™ are
trademarks of HarperCollins Publishers

FIRST EDITION
Designed by Joseph Rutt

Library of Congress Cataloging-in-Publication Data
Borg, Marcus J.
The last week : the day by day account of Jesus's final week in Jerusalem /
Marcus J. Borg and John Dominic Crossan. — 1st ed.
p. cm.
Includes bibliographical references.
ISBN-13: 978-0-06-084539-1
ISBN-10: 0-06-084539-2
1. Jesus Christ—Biography—Passion Week. 2. Bible. N.T. Mark—Criticism,
interpretaton, etc. I. Crossan, John Dominic. II. Title.
BT414.B67 2006
232.96—dc22 2005055148

06 07 08 09 10 RRD(H) 10 9 8 7 6 5 4 3 2 1

CONTENTS

———•◆•———

——— · ◆ · ———

THE FIRST
PASSION OF JESUS

This book is about the last week of Jesus's life. It is a week of extraordinary importance for Christians. With its climax on Good Friday and Easter, it is "Holy Week," the most sacred time of the Christian year. And because of its centrality for the lives of Christians, how this story is told matters greatly. What was the last week of Jesus's life about? And because this story is seen as revelatory, as speaking to us today, what *is* it about?

Two years ago, on Ash Wednesday at the beginning of Lent, Mel Gibson's movie *The Passion of the Christ* made the death of Jesus "big news" in the United States and elsewhere. Cover stories in national news magazines, prime-time television shows, and major stories in newspapers across the country featured the movie. Remarkable: almost two thousand years after it happened, the death of Jesus was once again front-page news. As the novelist Flannery O'Connor put it thirty years ago, we live in a "Christ-haunted" culture.

The movie was controversial and disclosed a division among contemporary Christians. Millions of Christians welcomed it enthusiastically and proclaimed it to have great potential for Christian evangelism in our time. Many were deeply moved by its graphic portrayal of how much suffering Jesus experienced "for us." Other Christians were disturbed by it—by its portrayal of "the Jews" and by its message that all of us were or are responsible for the death of Jesus: Jesus had to experience all of this horror because of us.

The movie had an additional effect. It reinforced a widespread but much too narrow understanding of the "passion" of Jesus. Mel Gibson called his film *The Passion of the Christ* and based his screenplay on Anne Catherine Emmerich's *The Dolorous Passion of Our Lord Jesus Christ*. Both authors understood the term "passion" in the context of its traditional Roman Catholic and broader Christian background. "Passion" is from the Latin noun *passio*, meaning "suffering."

But in everyday English we also use "passion" for any consuming interest, dedicated enthusiasm, or concentrated commitment. In this sense, a person's passion is what she or he is passionate about. In this book we are deliberately playing those two meanings against one another. The first passion of Jesus was the kingdom of God, namely, to incarnate the justice of God by demanding for all a fair share of a world belonging to and ruled by the covenantal God of Israel. It was that first passion for God's distributive justice that led inevitably to the second passion by Pilate's punitive justice. Before Jesus, after Jesus, and, for Christians, archetypically in Jesus, those who live for nonviolent justice die all too often from violent injustice. And so in this book we focus on "what Jesus was passionate about" as a way of understanding why his life ended in the passion of Good Friday. To narrow the passion of Jesus to his last twelve hours—arrest, trial, torture, and crucifixion—is to ignore the connection between his life and his death.

We do not in this book intend to attempt a historical reconstruction of Jesus's last week on earth. Our purpose is not to distinguish what actually happened from the way it is recorded in the four gospels, which proclaim it as "good news" (gospel). We intend a much simpler task: to tell and explain, against the background of Jewish high-priestly collaboration with Roman imperial control, the last week of Jesus's life on earth as given in the Gospel According to Mark. Both of us have spent our professional lives focused on the historical Jesus, but we work together here on this humbler task: to retell a story everyone thinks they know too well and most do not seem to know at all.

We have chosen Mark for two reasons. The first is that Mark is the earliest gospel, the first narrative account of Jesus's final week. Written some forty years after the life of Jesus, Mark tells us how the story of Jesus was told around the year 70. As such, it is not "straightforward history," but, like all the gospels, a combination of history remembered and history interpreted. It is the story of Jesus "updated" for the time in which Mark's community lived.

Scholarship of the past two hundred years has reached a fairly massive consensus not only that Mark was the first of the four New Testament gospels, but also that Matthew and Luke used it as their major source and that, quite probably, John used those earlier versions as his major source. In discussing Mark, therefore, we will also often refer to ways in which those later authors changed his version. This will be especially important where such changes have become better known than Mark's original version.

But there is also a second and equally important reason for choosing Mark. Namely, Mark alone went out of his way to chronicle Jesus's last week on a day-by-day basis, while the others kept some but not all of those indications of time. Here is what Mark says (with the addition of our day names):

Sunday: "When they were approaching Jerusalem" (11:1)

Monday: "On the following day" (11:12)

Tuesday: "In the morning" (11:20)

Wednesday: "It was two days before the Passover" (14:1)

Thursday: "On the first day of Unleavened Bread" (14:12)

Friday:	"As soon as it was morning" (15:1)
Saturday:	"The Sabbath" (15:42; 16:1)
Sunday:	"Very early on the first day of the week" (16:2)

Moreover, Mark alone also details "morning" and "evening" events for three of those days: Sunday (11:1, 11), Monday (11:12, 19), and Thursday (14:12, 17).

Finally, Mark alone chronicles Friday's events in careful three-hour intervals (like Roman military watch times):

6 AM	"As soon as it was morning" (15:1)
9 AM	"It was nine o'clock in the morning" (15:25)
12 noon	"When it was noon" (15:33)
3 PM	"At three o'clock" (15:34)
6 PM	"When evening had come" (15:42)

In other words, Mark alone has taken considerable care to tell his story so that hearers or readers can follow events day by day and eventually hour by hour. It seems almost a deliberate basis for a Holy Week liturgy that goes from Palm Sunday to Easter Sunday without skipping anything in between.

That last sentence introduces another major reason for this book. Christian liturgy has started to collapse Holy Week into its last three days and renamed Palm Sunday as Passion Sunday. On the one hand, Passion Sunday and Easter Sunday form a powerful dyad of death and resurrection. On the other, the loss of Palm Sunday's enthusiastic crowds and of all those days and events in between may weaken or even negate the meaning of that death and therefore of that resurrection. Our hope is that this slender volume may supply a needed corrective and proper narrative basis both for sacred liturgy within the church and for story, play, and film inside or outside it. Most especially, after two thousand years of theological anti-Judaism and even racial anti-Semitism derived from this story, it is time to read it again and get it right, to follow it closely and understand fully its narrative logic.

This book comes out of a friendship and a shared vocation. In some ways, we are an odd couple, and it is remarkable that our paths brought us together. Dom was born and raised in Ireland, Marcus in Minnesota and North Dakota. Dom grew up Catholic, Marcus grew up Lutheran (in a time when Lutherans were quite sure Catholics weren't really Christians). Dom became a monk and priest, Marcus married and had children. Dom taught for decades at a Catholic university in Chicago, Marcus at a public university in Oregon.

But then twenty years ago, Jesus brought us together. This is literally true. We met at an early meeting of the Jesus Seminar, and in the two decades since our friendship has grown. Even though we live at opposite ends of the country, the Borgs in Oregon, the Crossans in Florida, the four of us now spend many weeks together each year, in Oregon, Turkey, Ireland, Scotland, and elsewhere.

Our shared vocation is also centered on Jesus. It goes back a long way: both of us began our serious academic study of Jesus in our twenties. And though the jobs for which we were paid were in the academy, our passion for Jesus has always been more than academic. We have been, and are, passionate about the meaning of Jesus (and the Bible as a whole) for Christian life today. Our involvement with the sacred texts of our tradition has always been about, "What does *then* have to do with *now*?" And because we live in the United States, we are especially concerned with the question, "What does *then* have to do with *this* now, *our* now?"

We began this book by dividing between us the eight days of Jesus's last week on earth. We each wrote our own assignments without mutual consultation, so that what we had to unify in our editing were two independent interpretations of Mark's account.

We found ourselves concluding that process in early September 2005, not deliberately but most appropriately, along the banks of the Resurrection River, beside the shores of the Resurrection Bay, and in the reaches of the Resurrection Peninsula around Seward in south-central Alaska.

THE
LAST
WEEK

————◆————

ONE

————— ◆ —————

PALM SUNDAY

When they were approaching Jerusalem, at Bethphage and Bethany, near the Mount of Olives, he sent two of his disciples and said to them, "Go into the village ahead of you, and immediately as you enter it, you will find tied there a colt that has never been ridden; untie it and bring it. If anyone says to you, 'Why are you doing this?' just say this, 'The Lord needs it and will send it back here immediately.'" They went away and found a colt tied near a door, outside in the street. As they were untying it, some of the bystanders said to them, "What are you doing, untying the colt?" They told them what Jesus had said; and they allowed them to take it. Then they brought the colt to Jesus and threw their cloaks on it; and he sat on it. Many people spread their cloaks on the road, and others spread leafy branches that they had cut in the fields. Then those who went ahead and those who followed were shouting, "Hosanna! Blessed is the one who comes in the name of the Lord! Blessed is the coming kingdom of our ancestor David! Hosanna in the highest heaven!"

Then he entered Jerusalem and went into the temple; and when he had looked around at everything, as it was already late, he went out to Bethany with the twelve.

MARK 11:1–11

———— ◦ ————

Two processions entered Jerusalem on a spring day in the year 30. It was the beginning of the week of Passover, the most sacred week of the Jewish year. In the centuries since, Christians have celebrated this day as Palm Sunday, the first day of Holy Week. With its climax of Good Friday and Easter, it is the most sacred week of the Christian year.

One was a peasant procession, the other an imperial procession. From the east, Jesus rode a donkey down the Mount of Olives, cheered by his followers. Jesus was from the peasant village of Nazareth, his message was about the kingdom of God, and his followers came from the peasant class. They had journeyed to Jerusalem from Galilee, about a hundred miles to the north, a journey that is the central section and the central dynamic of Mark's gospel. Mark's story of Jesus and the kingdom of God has been aiming for Jerusalem, pointing toward Jerusalem. It has now arrived.

On the opposite side of the city, from the west, Pontius Pilate, the Roman governor of Idumea, Judea, and Samaria, entered Jerusalem at the head of a column of imperial cavalry and soldiers. Jesus's procession proclaimed the kingdom of God; Pilate's proclaimed the power of empire. The two processions embody the central conflict of the week that led to Jesus's crucifixion.

Pilate's military procession was a demonstration of both Roman imperial power and Roman imperial theology. Though unfamiliar to most people today, the imperial procession was well known in the Jewish homeland in the first century. Mark and the community for which he wrote would have known about it, for it was the standard practice of the Roman governors of Judea to be in Jerusalem for the major Jewish festivals. They did so not out of empathetic reverence for the religious devotion of their Jewish subjects, but to be in the city in case there was trouble. There often was, especially at Passover, a festival that celebrated the Jewish people's liberation from an earlier empire.

The mission of the troops with Pilate was to reinforce the Roman garrison permanently stationed in the Fortress Antonia, overlooking the Jewish temple and its courts. They and Pilate had come up from Caesarea Maritima, "Caesarea on the Sea," about sixty miles to the west. Like the Roman governors of Judea and Samaria before and after him, Pilate lived in the new and splendid city on the coast. For them, it was much more pleasant than Jerusalem, the traditional capital of the Jewish people, which was inland and insular, provincial and partisan, and often hostile. But for the major Jewish festivals, Pilate, like his predecessors and successors, went to Jerusalem.

Imagine the imperial procession's arrival in the city. A visual panoply of imperial power: cavalry on horses, foot soldiers, leather armor, helmets, weapons, banners, golden eagles mounted on poles, sun glinting on metal and gold. Sounds: the marching of feet, the creaking of leather, the clinking of bridles, the beating of drums. The swirling of dust. The eyes of the silent onlookers, some curious, some awed, some resentful.

Pilate's procession displayed not only imperial power, but also Roman imperial theology. According to this theology, the emperor was not simply the ruler of Rome, but the Son of God. It began with the greatest of the emperors, Augustus, who ruled Rome from 31 BCE to 14 CE. His father was the god Apollo, who conceived him in his mother, Atia. Inscriptions refer to him as "son of God," "lord" and "savior," one who had brought "peace on earth." After his death, he was seen ascending into heaven to take his permanent place among the gods. His successors continued to bear divine titles, including Tiberius, emperor from 14 to 37 CE and thus emperor during the time of Jesus's public activity. For Rome's Jewish subjects, Pilate's procession embodied not only a rival social order, but also a rival theology.

We return to the story of Jesus entering Jerusalem. Although it is familiar, it has surprises. As Mark tells the story in 11:1–11, it is a prearranged "counterprocession." Jesus planned it in advance. As

Jesus approaches the city from the east at the end of the journey from Galilee, he tells two of his disciples to go to the next village and get him a colt they will find there, one that has never been ridden, that is, a young one. They do so, and Jesus rides the colt down the Mount of Olives to the city surrounded by a crowd of enthusiastic followers and sympathizers, who spread their cloaks, strew leafy branches on the road, and shout, "Hosanna! Blessed is the one who comes in the name of the Lord! Blessed is the coming kingdom of our ancestor David! Hosanna in the highest heaven!" As one of our professors in graduate school said about forty years ago, this looks like a planned political demonstration.[1]

The meaning of the demonstration is clear, for it uses symbolism from the prophet Zechariah in the Jewish Bible. According to Zechariah, a king would be coming to Jerusalem (Zion) "humble, and riding on a colt, the foal of a donkey" (9:9). In Mark, the reference to Zechariah is implicit. Matthew, when he treats Jesus's entry into Jerusalem, makes the connection explicit by quoting the passage: "Tell the daughter of Zion, look, your king is coming to you, humble, and mounted on a donkey, and on a colt, the foal of a donkey (Matt. 21:5, quoting Zech. 9:9).[2] The rest of the Zechariah passage details what *kind* of king he will be:

> He will cut off the chariot from Ephraim and the war-horse from Jerusalem; and the battle bow shall be cut off, and he shall command peace to the nations. (9:10)

This king, riding on a donkey, will banish war from the land—no more chariots, war-horses, or bows. Commanding peace to the nations,[3] he will be a king of peace.

Jesus's procession deliberately countered what was happening on the other side of the city. Pilate's procession embodied the power, glory, and violence of the empire that ruled the world. Jesus's procession embodied an alternative vision, the kingdom of God. This contrast—between the kingdom of God and the kingdom of Caesar—is central not only to the gospel of Mark, but to the story of Jesus and early Christianity.

The confrontation between these two kingdoms continues through the last week of Jesus's life. As we all know, the week ends with Jesus's execution by the powers who ruled his world. Holy Week is the story of this confrontation. But before we unfold Mark's story of Jesus's last week, we must first set the stage. For this, Jerusalem is central.

JERUSALEM

Jerusalem was not just any city. By the first century, it had been the center of the sacred geography of the Jewish people for a millennium. And ever since, it has been central to the sacred imagination of both Jews and Christians. Its associations are both positive and negative. It is the city of God and the faithless city, the city of hope and the city of oppression, the city of joy and the city of pain.

Jerusalem became the capital of ancient Israel in the time of King David, around 1000 BCE. Under David and his son Solomon, Israel experienced the greatest period in its history. The country was united, all twelve tribes under one king; it was at its largest; it was powerful and thus its people were safe from marauding neighbors; a glorious temple was built by Solomon in Jerusalem. David's reign in particular (and not Solomon's) was seen not only as a time of power and glory, but also of justice and righteousness in the land. David was the just and righteous king. He became associated with goodness, power, protection, and justice; he was the ideal shepherd-king, the apple of God's eye, even God's son.

The time of glory, the ideal time, was remembered. So revered did David become that the hoped-for future deliverer, the messiah, was expected to be a "son of David," a new David, indeed greater than David. And this new David, this son of David, would rule a restored kingdom from Jerusalem. Jerusalem was thus associated with Israel's hope of future glory—a glory involving justice and peace as much or more than it involved power.

David's son Solomon built the temple in Jerusalem in the 900s BCE. It became the sacred center of the Jewish world. Within the theology that developed around it, it was the "navel of the earth" connecting this world to its source in God, and here (and only here) was God's dwelling place on earth. Of course, ancient Israel also affirmed that God was everywhere. Heaven and the highest heaven could not contain God, and God's glory filled the earth, but God was especially present in the temple. To be in the temple was to be in God's presence.

The temple mediated not only God's presence, but also God's forgiveness. In was the only place of sacrifice, and sacrifice was the means of forgiveness. According to temple theology, some sins could be forgiven and some kinds of impurities could be dealt with only through temple sacrifice. As the mediator of forgiveness and purification, the temple mediated access to God. To stand in the temple, purified and forgiven, was to stand in the presence of God.

The temple was thus a center of devotion and the destination of pilgrimage. The devotion evoked by Jerusalem is movingly expressed in a collection of psalms (Pss. 120–34) used by Jewish pilgrims as they "went up" to Jerusalem on pilgrimage. Commonly called "songs of ascent," they speak of the yearning and joy engendered by Jerusalem as the city of God (the "house of the Lord" is the temple):

> I was glad when they said to me,
> "Let us go to the house of the Lord!"
> Our feet are standing within your gates, O Jerusalem. . . .
> Pray for the peace of Jerusalem:
> "May they prosper who love you."

When the Lord restored the fortunes of Zion,
we were like those who dream.
Then our mouth was filled with laughter,
and our tongue with shouts of joy.

For the Lord has chosen Zion;
God has desired it for God's habitation:
"This is my resting place forever;
here I will reside, for I have desired it."
(Pss. 122:1–2, 6; 126:1–2; 132:13–14)

But Jerusalem the city of God also acquired negative associations, because, beginning in the half century after King David, it became the center of a "domination system." Because this notion is so important for understanding a conflict that runs through the Bible as a whole and the last week of Jesus's life in particular, we pause here to explain it.

The phrase "domination system" is shorthand for the most common form of social system—a way of organizing a society—in ancient and premodern times, that is, in preindustrial agrarian societies. It names a social system marked by three major features:

1. Political oppression. In such societies the many were ruled by the few, the powerful and wealthy elites: the monarchy, nobility, aristocracy, and their associates. Ordinary people had no voice in the shaping of the society.

2. Economic exploitation. A high percentage of the society's wealth, which came primarily from agricultural production in preindustrial societies, went into the coffers of the wealthy and powerful—between one-half and two-thirds of it. How did they manage to do this? By the way they set the system up, through the structures and laws about land ownership, taxation, indenture of labor through debt, and so forth.

3. Religious legitimation. In ancient societies, these systems
were legitimated, or justified, with religious language. The
people were told the king ruled by divine right, the king was
the Son of God, the social order reflected the will of God,
and the powers that be were ordained by God. Of course,
religion sometimes became the source of protest against
these claims. But in most premodern societies known to us,
religion has been used to legitimate the place of the wealthy
and powerful in the social order over which they preside.

There is nothing unusual about this form of society. Monar-
chical and aristocratic rule by a wealthy few began about five
thousand years ago and was the most common form of social system in the ancient world. With various permutations, it persisted
through the medieval and early modern periods until the demo-
cratic revolutions of the last few hundred years. And one could
make a good case that in somewhat different form it remains
with us today.

In this sense "domination systems" are normal, not abnormal,
and thus can also be called the "normalcy of civilization." Thus we
will use both phrases to name the socio-economic-political order
in which ancient Israel, Jesus, and early Christianity lived. "Domination system" calls attention to its central dynamic: the political
and economic domination of the many by a few and the use of religious claims to justify it. The religious version is that God has
set society up this way; the secular version is that this is "the way
things are" and the best they can be for everybody. "Normalcy of
civilization" calls attention to how common it is. There is nothing
unusual or abnormal about this state of affairs. It is what most
commonly happens.

We return to the emergence of this social system in ancient
Israel. Under David's son and successor Solomon, power and
wealth were increasingly concentrated in Jerusalem. In effect,
Solomon had become a new Pharaoh and Egypt had been re-

created in Israel.[4] And though Israel split into two kingdoms when Solomon died in 922 BCE (the Northern Kingdom, Israel; and the Southern Kingdom, Judah, with its capital in Jerusalem), the domination system persisted through the remaining centuries of the monarchy. And, as we suggest later in this chapter, it was the form of social system confronted by Jesus and early Christianity.

The negative associations of Jerusalem are especially strong in the prophets of ancient Israel, whose words by the time of Jesus were part of the Jewish Bible. As the home of the monarchy and aristocracy, of wealth and power, Jerusalem became the center of injustice and of betrayal of God's covenant. God's passion for justice had been replaced by human injustice.

To illustrate, we begin with Micah, an eighth-century BCE prophet. He asks, What is the sin of Judah? His surprising answer takes the form of a rhetorical question, "Is it not Jerusalem?" (1:5). It is a striking claim: the sin of Judah is a *city*, indeed the city of God. His indictment of the rulers is explicit:

> Listen, you heads of Jacob and rulers of the house of Israel! Should you not know justice?—you who hate the good and love the evil, who tear the skin off my people, and the flesh off their bones.... Hear this, you rulers ... who abhor justice and pervert all equity, who build Zion with blood and Jerusalem with wrong! (3:1–2, 9–10)

In the same century, the prophet Isaiah indicted the rulers of Jerusalem as "rulers of Sodom" and its inhabitants as "people of Gomorrah," two ancient cities legendary for their injustice (1:10). His language is shocking and harsh:

> How the faithful city has become a whore! She that was full of justice, righteousness lodged in her—but now murderers!... Your princes are rebels and companions of thieves. Everyone loves a bribe and runs after gifts. They do not

defend the orphan, and the widow's cause does not come before them. (1:21, 23)

At the conclusion of his parable of the vineyard, Isaiah said about the beloved but faithless city: "God expected justice, but saw bloodshed, righteousness, but heard a cry!" (5:7). To its rulers, he said: "You call evil good and good evil, who put darkness for light and light for darkness, who put bitter for sweet, and sweet for bitter!" (5:20).

The same themes sound in the late seventh- and early-sixth century BCE prophet Jeremiah:

Run to and fro through the streets of Jerusalem, look around and take note! Search its squares and see if you can find one person who acts justly and seeks truth. . . . Has this house [the temple], which is called by God's name, become a den of robbers? . . . This is the city that must be punished; there is nothing but oppression within her. (5:1; 7:11; 6:6)

Yet even among the prophets who indicted it so sharply, Jerusalem also retained positive associations as the city of God and city of hope. As we have already briefly mentioned, its greatest king, David, was a model for a hoped-for future messiah. Moreover, Jerusalem's future was not just about itself; rather, it was a hope for the world, God's dream for the world.

In one of the most famous passages from the Hebrew Bible, Isaiah describes Jerusalem as a source of instruction in righteousness for the whole world:

In days to come the mountain of the Lord's house [the temple] shall be established as the highest of the mountains and shall be raised above the hills; all the nations shall stream to it. Many peoples shall come and say, "Come, let us go up to the mountain of the Lord, to the house of the God of Jacob; that God may teach us God's ways and that we may walk in God's paths." For out of Zion shall go forth instruction, and the word of the Lord from Jerusalem. (2:2–3)

The result will be a world of peace:

They shall beat their swords into plowshares, and their spears into pruning hooks. Nation shall not lift up sword against nation, neither shall they learn war any more. (2:4)

The last passage is also found in Micah (4:1–3), but with an addition. After the verses promising a world of peace, Micah adds: "They shall all sit under their own vines and under their own fig trees, and no one shall make them afraid" (4:4).[5] These are images of justice, prosperity, and security. Justice: everyone will have their own land. Prosperity: vines and fig trees are about more than subsistence survival. Security: they will not have to live in a state of constant fear. And the creation of this world of justice and peace, in which fear will be no more, will come from the God whose dwelling place is Jerusalem.

JERUSALEM IN THE CENTURIES BEFORE JESUS

It was the prophets' warnings and not their hope that came to pass. After a dreadful siege of over a year, Jerusalem was conquered by the Babylonians in 586 BCE. The city and the temple were destroyed, and many of the Jewish survivors of the war were taken into exile in Babylon, where they lived in conditions of virtual slavery. It looked like the end of the Jewish people.

But even in exile, the yearning for Jerusalem remained. In Psalm 137 are poignant words filled with grief and resolve:

By the rivers of Babylon, there we sat down and there we wept when we remembered Zion.

On the willows there we hung up our harps.
For there our captors asked us for songs,
and our tormentors asked for mirth, saying,
"Sing us one of the songs of Zion."

How could we sing the Lord's song in a foreign land?
If I forget you, O Jerusalem, let my right hand wither!
Let my tongue cling to the roof of my mouth,
  if I do not remember you,
  if I do not set Jerusalem above my highest joy. (137:1–6)

After about fifty years in exile, the Jewish people were permitted to return to their homeland. In the late 500s, within a few decades of their return, they rebuilt the temple. Because of the impoverished state of the returned community, it was a very modest structure compared to the temple of Solomon, which had been destroyed.

For several centuries Judea with its capital in Jerusalem was ruled by foreign empires. Under the Persian Empire and its Hellenistic successors, the temple in Jerusalem was the center of local government in Judea. The high priest and the temple authorities were in effect the rulers of the Jewish people, though of course they owed allegiance and tribute to their imperial overlords. This state of affairs continued into the second century BCE, when the Jewish people gained their independence from the Hellenistic empire of Antiochus Epiphanes around 164 BCE. The successful revolt was led by a Jewish family known as the Maccabees. Also known as the Hasmoneans, they ruled the Jewish homeland from Jerusalem for about a hundred years, until it fell under the control of Rome in 63 BCE.

After abolishing the Jewish monarchy, Rome initially ruled through the high priest, the temple, and a local aristocracy centered in the temple. This was Rome's traditional practice throughout its territory: appointing local collaborators from the indigenous population to rule on Rome's behalf. The primary qualification was wealth—Rome trusted wealthy families. These local collaborators were given a relatively free hand in their rule of their own population, so long as they were loyal to Rome and maintained order. There was one additional condition: they were responsible for collecting and paying the annual tribute owed to Rome.

However, in the decades after Rome took control of the Jewish homeland, there were power struggles among the Jewish aristocratic families, and so Rome appointed as king of the Jews a man named Herod, an Idumean whose family had only recently converted to Judaism. Herod had a long reign, until 4 BCE, and eventually became known to history as Herod the Great.

Herod was obviously a man of great ability, though also ruthless. Early in his reign, he ordered the execution of many of the traditional aristocracy in order to secure himself against power struggles and also perhaps to confiscate their land and wealth. He thereby eliminated the old elites of wealth and power and replaced them with new elites who owed their position to him. He did not trust his subjects and placed them under surveillance, prohibiting unauthorized public gatherings. He also severely limited the power of the high priest. Though according to Jewish law, the high priest was to serve for life, Herod appointed and deposed seven high priests during his thirty-three years as king. Moreover, he restricted their role to their narrowly religious function in the temple.

Herod ruled from Jerusalem, and the city became magnificent during his reign. Above all, he rebuilt the temple. Beginning in the 20s of the first century BCE, Herod "remodeled" the modest postexilic temple, but in effect built a new temple surrounded by spacious courts and elegant colonnades, with sumptuous use of marble and gold. To do so, he had first to construct an enormous platform, about 1,550 feet by 1,000 feet—almost 40 acres. Even non-Jewish writers described the temple complex as the most magnificent in the Roman Empire.

He built a palace for himself, which was later to become the residence of the Roman governors, including Pilate, when they were in Jerusalem. It was luxurious, with columns of colored marble and glittering fountains, shaded pools, ceilings painted with gold and vermillion, chairs of silver and gold inlaid with jewels, mosaic floors with agate and lapis lazuli. Like the temple, it was huge. His dining room had enough couches for three hundred guests.[6]

Herod's building projects went beyond Jerusalem. On the coast, he built a huge all-weather port on Judea's Mediterranean coast at Caesarea Maritima, later to become the center of Roman administration in the Jewish homeland. The city was named after Caesar and the harbor after Augustus (Sebastos in Greek). The harbor's giant breakwaters had foundations using state-of-the-art cement that dried under water, and they were large enough to support huge warehouses. Through its triple anchorages passed not just trade and commerce, but pilgrimage and tourism. He also built fortresses and palaces for himself at Masada, Herodium, Jericho, and Machareus. Inside and outside of his kingdom, he financed the building of temples to Caesar Augustus.

All of this cost an enormous amount of money. In addition to paying for his building projects and his opulent lifestyle, he was responsible for collecting and paying annual tribute to Rome. His sources of income were the ones available to rulers in preindustrial agrarian societies: direct ownership of agricultural land (royal lands), taxation, and, for want of a better word, extortion from wealthy families whom he had favored.

Though history knows him as "Herod the Great," he was not popular with many Jews. Some called him "Herod the Monstrous." He was profligate in his spending, brutal in his oppression, and near the end of his reign psychopathically paranoid.

Indeed, when he died in 4 BCE, revolts erupted throughout his kingdom. So serious were they that Roman legions had to be brought south from Syria to quell them. In Galilee, the Romans burned and destroyed the city of Sepphoris, four miles from Nazareth, and sold many of the survivors into slavery. After Jerusalem was retaken, the Romans crucified two thousand of its defenders en masse. The suppression of the revolts of 4 BCE was the first direct Jewish experience of Roman military power in several decades.

Herod had ruled the whole of the Jewish homeland. After his death, Rome divided his kingdom into three parts, each ruled by one of his sons. Galilee and trans-Jordanian Perea were assigned to Herod Antipas, the area northeast of the Jordan to Philip, and Judea and Samaria to Archelaus. Like his father, Archelaus ruled from Jerusalem. But in 6 CE, Rome removed Archelaus from his throne and began to rule his portion of Herod's kingdom with governors sent from Rome.

JERUSALEM IN THE FIRST CENTURY

The events of 6 CE significantly changed political circumstances for Jerusalem and the temple. Rome continued its practice of placing local administration under rulers chosen from local elites, and with Archelaus gone, Rome assigned this role to the temple and its authorities. Though the temple had always been religiously important, it now became the central economic and political institution in the country.

The temple replaced Herodian rule as the center of the local domination system. A domination system was not new—it had existed under Herod and before. What was new was that the temple was now at the center of local collaboration with Rome. It had the defining features of ancient domination systems: *rule by a few, economic exploitation,* and *religious legitimation.* And it was a two-layered domination system: the local domination system centered in the temple was subsumed under the imperial domination system that was Roman rule. As such, it owed "tribute" to the emperor, both loyalty and money, and was thus a tributary domination system.

The *few* who *ruled* at the top of the local system were the temple authorities, headed by the high priest, including members of aristocratic families. Mark's terminology for the temple authorities is "the chief priests, the elders, and the scribes" (e.g., 14:53). The chief priests came from high-ranking priestly families and the elders from wealthy lay families. Many would have been from the new elites recently created by Herod. The scribes associated with "chief priests" and "elders" were a literate class who worked for them as legal experts, record keepers, and lower-level administrators. Mark also refers to a "council," a governing body in Jerusalem composed largely or completely of these groups.

With regard to *economic* conditions, the temple authorities, priestly and lay, came from wealthy families. Because wealth in the premodern world was primarily the product of land ownership and the agricultural production that comes from it, many were large landowners. Even many high-priestly families owned land, despite the Jewish law's prohibition of ownership of land by priests. (Their scribes interpreted the prohibition to mean that they could not work on the land, though they could own it; as you think about it, this is what one would expect.) Because they lived in Jerusalem away from their lands, they were also absentee landlords. In this they were typical, for wealthy landowners most often lived in cities.

In order to accumulate land, the wealthy, whether lay or priestly, had to subvert laws about land in the Jewish Bible. Among those laws was one that said agricultural land could not be bought or sold. The reason for the law was to try to ensure that every family had its own plot of land in perpetuity. Thus land could be acquired only by confiscation, which occurred in at least two forms. First, land could be confiscated by a king. Herod had large "royal estates," royal lands, and presumably he didn't buy all these. He also gave land to the new elites he created. Indeed, having land is what made them elites.

The second form of land acquisition by confiscation was foreclosure because of debt. Though land could not be bought or sold, it could be used as collateral for a loan. Then, if the loan was not repaid, the land could be confiscated. It is not difficult to see how this benefited the wealthy: only peasant families struggling for short-term survival, in desperate straits, whether from a bad crop year or other reasons, would mortgage their land. The foreclosure rate would have been high, for the struggling peasant families would have then been be in debt as well.[7]

These are the two primary ways that powerful and wealth elites acquired land (and thus more wealth). Once they owned the land, they could also decide what to do with it—whether to allow the previous owners to stay on as tenants or whether to replace them with sharecroppers or day laborers. And because larger estates often shifted agricultural production from basic products (grains, vegetables, and so forth) to more specialized products (figs, dates, olives, and so forth), many former owners were displaced. Thus the loss of land meant not only becoming somebody else's laborer, but also that the land was no longer the source of family food subsistence. These people no longer produced the basics, but instead had to buy them.

There are persuasive reasons for thinking that this process of peasant displacement through the growth of large estates during the Herodian and Roman period was accelerating. The reign of Herod brought an explosion of large estates and concentration of wealth, and this process continued into the first century. The conditions of peasant life were worsening.

The integration of Jewish Palestine into the Roman Empire brought about the commercialization of agriculture, with the effects just mentioned: there was a dramatic rise in the number of large landowners; peasants were forced off their ancestral land, where for centuries they had produced what they needed for their

families; subsistence farming was replaced with agricultural production for sale and export. Peasants who had owned their own
land became tenant farmers or sharecroppers, and the owners of
large estates sought to work the land with as few tenants as possible. Landless peasants had few options: day labor, emigration,
working on building projects in a city, begging. Though by modern Western standards peasant existence had always been meager,
it had been adequate. Now, for many, it no longer was.

Jerusalem was not only the home of large landowners who received wealth from their estates. Wealth flowed into the city for
other reasons. The temple was the center of both a local and an
imperial tax system. The local taxes, commonly called "tithes,"
were on agricultural production. Most tithes were paid to the
temple and priesthood, and the rest were to be spent in Jerusalem. The tithes amounted to over 20 percent of production.
There was also an annual "temple tax" paid by Jewish men over a
certain age, including millions of Jews living in the Diaspora,
Jewish communities in other lands. And, beginning in 6 CE, the
temple and temple authorities were also the center of the imperial
tax system. They had the responsibility for collecting and paying
the annual tribute due to Rome. Also, as the economic center of
the domination system, records of debt were stored in the temple.

Wealth poured into the city for yet another reason. Hundreds
of thousands of Jewish pilgrims visited the city each year. Though
population estimates for cities in the ancient world are difficult,
Jerusalem probably had around forty thousand inhabitants in the
first century. But for a major festival like Passover, two hundred
thousand pilgrims or more would come to the city. Moreover,
non-Jewish travelers were also attracted to Jerusalem, commonly
described as one of the most beautiful cities in the ancient Near
East.

Jerusalem's elites lived in luxury. One would expect this, and
recent archaeology in Jerusalem has confirmed it by unearthing
one of their villas. The remains point to the opulence of the upper

class. Their wealth attests to their position at the top of a domination system under which the economic condition of the peasant class was declining.

Importantly, the issue as we describe the wealthy and powerful is not whether they—in our case, the Jerusalem authorities centered in the temple—were "corrupt," if by that we mean an individual failing. As individuals, the wealthy and powerful can be good people—responsible, honest, hard-working, faithful to family and friends, interesting, charming, and good-hearted. The issue is not their individual virtue or wickedness, but the role they played in the domination system. They shaped it, enforced it, and benefited from it.

The high priest and the temple authorities had a difficult task. As with the client-rulers before them, their primary obligation to Rome was loyalty and collaboration. They were to make sure that the annual tribute to Rome was paid. They were also to maintain domestic peace and order. Rome did not want rebellions. Their role was to be the intermediaries between a local domination system and an imperial domination system.

It was a delicate balancing act. They needed to collaborate enough with Rome to keep Rome happy, but not so much as to anger their Jewish subjects. They were in an awkward spot. Their decisions were often difficult. It is easy to imagine a responsible official saying, as the high priest Caiaphas is reported to have said in John's gospel, "It is better to have one man die for the people than to have the whole nation destroyed" (11:50). Why Caiaphas says this can be seen from a previous verse that shows a fear of Roman intervention: "If we let him go on like this, everyone will believe in him, and the Romans will come and destroy both our holy place and our nation" (11:48).

Some high priests seem to have been more successful walking this tightrope than others. Though Jewish law mandated that the high priest was to serve for life, as mentioned earlier, Rome replaced high priests with great frequency. There were eighteen high priests from the time Rome shifted local rule from Archelaus to the temple in 6 CE to the outbreak of the great revolt in 66 CE. Caiaphas, the high priest during Jesus's public activity, must have been particularly skillful, for he held the office for eighteen years, from 18 to about 36 CE.

The temple's role as the center of a domination system was *legitimated by theology:* its place in the system was said to have been given by God. Temple theology continued to see the temple as the dwelling place of God, the mediator of forgiveness through sacrifice, the center of devotion, and the destination of pilgrimage.

It is important to emphasize once again that there is nothing abnormal about all of this. It was (is?) exceedingly common in all of its permutations. The wealthy and powerful justify their position by saying, "This is the way it is." Whether done by religious or nonreligious authorities, the effect is the same. God—or the way things work—has set it up this way.

This is the Jerusalem that Jesus entered on Palm Sunday. His message was deeply critical of the temple and its role in the domination system, as we shall see.

Jesus was not the only Jewish anti-temple voice in the first century. Given the temple's role in a tributary domination system collaborating with an imperial domination system, this should not be surprising. Among the other voices were the Essenes, almost certainly to be identified with the community that produced the Dead Sea Scrolls. They rejected the legitimacy of the present temple and priesthood, understood their own community to be an interim temple, and looked forward to the day when they would be restored to power in a purified temple in Jerusalem.

Much of the passion of violent Jewish revolutionary movements was directed against Jerusalem and the temple because of its collaboration with the domination system. The great Jewish revolt that broke out in 66 CE was directed as much against the Jewish collaborators in Jerusalem as it was against Rome itself.

When the Jewish rebels, by then known as "Zealots," took Jerusalem at the beginning of the revolt, their first acts were to replace the high priest with a new high priest chosen by lot from the peasant class and to burn the records of debt housed in the temple.

In the gospels, the movements of both John the Baptizer and Jesus had an anti-temple dimension. John's baptism was for the "forgiveness of sins." But forgiveness was a function that temple theology claimed for itself, mediated by sacrifice in the temple. For John to proclaim forgiveness apart from the temple was to deny the temple's role as the essential mediator of forgiveness and access to God.

Like John, Jesus pronounced forgiveness apart from temple sacrifice. It is implicit in much of his activity, including his eating with "tax collectors and sinners," who were seen as intrinsically impure, but it becomes explicit as well. For example, in Mark 2, Jesus forgives the sins of a paralyzed man and empowers him to walk. Some scribes object: "Why does this fellow speak in this way? It is blasphemy. Who can forgive sins but God alone?" (2:7). Their point is not that Jesus is claiming to be God. Rather, their point is that God has provided a way to forgive sins—namely, through temple sacrifice. And here is Jesus, like John, proclaiming forgiveness apart from the temple.

Other teachings of Jesus reflect both the positive and negative associations of the temple and Jerusalem. On the one hand, Jerusalem is "the city of the great King" (Matt. 5:35) and the object of God's love: "How often have I desired to gather your children together as a hen gathers her brood under her wings." And yet, as the same passage continues, Jerusalem is "the city that kills the prophets and stones those who are sent to it" (Matt. 23:37; Luke 13:34). In another passage, reported only in Luke, Jesus weeps over the city even as, like one of the classical prophets of ancient Israel, he indicts it:

As Jesus drew near and saw Jerusalem, he wept over it, saying, "If you, even you, had only recognized the things that
make for peace! But now they are hidden from your eyes.
Indeed, the days will come upon you, when your enemies
will set up ramparts around you and surround you, and hem
you in on every side. They will crush you to the ground, you
and your children within you, and they will not leave within
you one stone upon another, because you did not recognize
the time of your visitation from God." (19:41–44)

Thus in these voices from the time of Jesus, Jerusalem with its
temple was still seen as "the city of God" that called forth Jewish
devotion. But it was also the center of a local domination system,
the center of the ruling class, the center of great wealth, and the
center of collaboration with Rome.

Jerusalem and the temple did not survive the first century. In
the year 70 CE, Roman legions shattered the great revolt by recon-
quering the city. When they had done so, they tore down the
temple, leaving only part of the western wall of the temple platform. The destruction of the temple changed Judaism forever.
Sacrifice ceased, the role of the priesthood was eclipsed, and the
central institutions of Judaism became scripture and synagogue.

The gospel of Mark was written very near the time of the
temple's destruction. Mainline scholars date it no earlier than 65,
and most say "around 70," a range from a few years before the
temple's destruction to a few years after. In either case, Jerusalem
was very much "in the news" when Mark wrote. Mark is, as one
of our colleagues puts it, "a wartime gospel."[8]

JERUSALEM IN THE GOSPEL OF MARK

Jerusalem is central to Mark's story of Jesus. Even before the
gospel reaches its climax in Jerusalem, it is the central dynamic of
the gospel. Six of Mark's sixteen chapters are set in Jerusalem, al-

most 40 percent of the whole (in Matthew, 33 percent, and in Luke, just over 20 percent). If we add the central section of Mark that tells the story of Jesus's final journey to Jerusalem, it is the theme of over half of his gospel. But before developing the role of Jerusalem in Mark's story, we need to say something about the Jesus of Mark's gospel and his message.

In Mark, Jesus's message is not about *himself*—not about his identity as the Messiah, the Son of God, the Lamb of God, the Light of the World, or any of the other exalted terms familiar to Christians. Of course, Mark affirms that Jesus is both the Messiah and the Son of God; he tells us so in the opening verse of the gospel: "The beginning of the good news of Jesus Christ, the Son of God."

But this is not part of Jesus's own message. He neither proclaims nor teaches this, nor does this form part of his followers' teaching during his lifetime. Rather, in Mark only voices from the Spirit world speak of Jesus's special identity. At his baptism, "a voice from heaven" declares, "You are my Son, the Beloved; with you I am well pleased" (1:11). The voice is addressed to Jesus alone ("You"); nobody else hears it. At his transfiguration, the same voice speaks, but now to his disciples. The first half of the declaration is the same, but now it is in the third person: "This is my Son, the Beloved." The second half reads: "Listen to him" (9:7). So also evil spirits know who he is. "Unclean" spirits exclaim, "I know who you are, the Holy One of God," "You are the Son of God," and "What have you to do with me, Jesus, Son of the Most High God?" (1:24; 3:11; 5:7). But these declarations are not heard by the disciples or by other people; no reaction is reported.

On only two occasions does Jesus seem to affirm an exalted identity for himself. But they are not part of his message; both are in private, not in public. And we say "seem" because both stories are ambiguous. The first is the well-known story of Peter's confession of faith at the end of the first half of Mark. In response to Jesus's question to his disciples, "Who do people say that I am?"

Peter says, "You are the Messiah." This is the only time in Mark's gospel that a follower of Jesus says anything like this. Jesus's response confirms that this has not been part of Jesus's own message: "And he sternly ordered them not to tell anyone about him" (8:27–30).[9]

The second occasion is very near the end of the gospel. On the night before his execution, Jesus is interrogated by the high priest, who asks him, "Are you the Messiah, the Son of the Blessed One?" The response of Jesus is commonly translated "I am" (14:61–62), but in Greek, the language in which Mark writes, the phrase is ambiguous. Greek does not reverse word order to indicate a question rather than a statement. Thus Jesus's response, *ego eimi*, can mean either "I am" or "Am I?" As Matthew and Luke revise this scene from Mark, they treat Jesus's response as other than a straightforward affirmation. Matthew changes it to "You have said so," and Luke to "You say that I am" (Matt. 26:64; Luke 22:70), suggesting that there may be a basis for translating the phrase as a question.

If Jesus's message in Mark was not about himself, what was it about? For Mark, it is about the *kingdom of God* and the *way*. To begin with the latter, the opening verses of the gospel proclaim that it is about the "way": "See, I am sending my messenger ahead of you, who will prepare your *way*; the voice of one crying out in the wilderness, 'Prepare the *way* of the Lord'" (1:2–3). The Greek word for "way" is *hodos*, and Mark uses it frequently throughout his gospel. Its frequency is somewhat obscured in English, for *hodos* is translated with a number of words: "way," "road," "path." Behind them all is *hodos*, the "way."

And Jesus's message is about the kingdom of God. Mark signals its centrality by making it his advance summary of Jesus's message. In Mark, the first words of Jesus's public activity, his "inaugural address," are: "The time is fulfilled, and the kingdom of God has come near" (1:15). Because of its importance for seeing Mark's portrait of Jesus, we shall linger on it.

"Kingdom of God" is a political as well as religious metaphor. Religiously, it is the kingdom of *God;* politically, it is the *kingdom* of God. In the first century, "kingdom" was a political term. Jesus's hearers (and Mark's community) knew of and lived under kingdoms: the kingdoms of Herod and his sons, the kingdom of Rome. Jesus could have spoken of the family of God, the community of God, or the people of God, but, according to Mark, he spoke of the *kingdom* of God. To his hearers, it would have suggested a kingdom very different from the kingdoms they knew, very different from the domination systems that ruled their lives. And Jesus's message in Mark, as we will suggest later, is about the *already present kingdom of God* that is also yet to come in its fullness.

Mark concludes his advance summary of Jesus's message with, "Repent, and believe in the good news" (1:15). The word "repent" has two meanings here, both quite different from the later Christian meaning of contrition for sin. From the Hebrew Bible, it has the meaning of "to return," especially "to return from exile," an image also associated with "way," "path," and "journey." The roots of the Greek word for "repent" mean "to go beyond the mind that you have." To repent is to embark upon a way that goes beyond the mind that you have. So also the word "believe" has a meaning quite different from the common Christian understanding. For Christians, "to believe" often means thinking that a set of statements, a set of doctrines, is true. But the ancient meaning of the word "believe" has much more to do with trust and commitment. "To believe in the good news," as Mark puts it, means to trust in the news that the kingdom of God is near and to commit to that kingdom.

And to whom did Jesus direct his message about the kingdom of God and the "way"? Primarily to *peasants.* As we use the term, it is a large social category that includes not only agricultural laborers, but the rural population as a whole in preindustrial agrarian societies. Mark does not report the condition of the peasant class. He did not need to, for he and his community were well aware of it. About 90 percent of the population was rural, living on farms or in hamlets, villages, and small towns. The rural population was the primary producer of wealth; by definition, there was no industry, and "manufacturing" was done by hand by artisans, also part of the peasant class. As already mentioned briefly, cities were the home of the wealthy and powerful, along with their "retainers" (their employees) and merchants (and their employees) who served the wealthy class.

In Mark (and the other gospels), Jesus never goes to a city (except Jerusalem, of course). Though the first half of Mark is set in Galilee, Mark does not report that Jesus went to its largest cities, Sepphoris and Tiberias, even though the first is only four miles from Nazareth and the second is on the shore of the Sea of Galilee, the area of most of Jesus's activity. Instead, Jesus speaks in the countryside and in small towns like Capernaum. Why? The most compelling answer is that Jesus saw his message as to and for peasants.

According to Mark, Jesus's message and activity immediately involved him in conflict with authorities. Chapters 2 and 3 contain a series of conflict stories; his opponents are named as scribes, Pharisees, and Herodians (2:1–3:6). Near the end of these stories, the first explicit reference to Jerusalem occurs. Scribes "who came down from Jerusalem" accuse Jesus of being possessed: "He has Beelzebul, and by the ruler of the demons he casts out demons" (3:22).

Jerusalem becomes central in the section of Mark that tells the story of Jesus's journey from Galilee to Jerusalem. It begins roughly halfway through Mark with Peter's affirmation that Jesus is the Messiah. The next two and a half chapters, leading to Jesus's entry into Jerusalem on Palm Sunday, are about what it means to follow Jesus, to be a genuine disciple. Mark develops this theme by weaving together several subthemes:

- Following Jesus means following him on *the way*.
- *The way* leads to Jerusalem.
- Jerusalem is the place of *confrontation with the authorities*.
- Jerusalem is the place of *death and resurrection*.

Immediately after Mark reports Peter's affirmation that Jesus is the Messiah, Jesus for the first time speaks of his destiny. He is going to Jerusalem, where he will be executed by the authorities:

Then Jesus began to teach his disciples that the Son of Man must undergo great suffering, and be rejected by the elders, the chief priests, and the scribes, and be killed, and after three days rise again. (8:31)

Commonly called the "first prediction of the passion," it is followed by two more solemn announcements anticipating Jesus's execution that structure this part of Mark. The themes of confrontation with authorities and execution and resurrection toll like a death knell. The second announcement is one chapter later:

The Son of Man is to be betrayed into human hands, and they will kill him, and three days after being killed, he will rise again. (9:31)

A chapter later, it sounds for a third time. Jesus and his followers "were *on the road* [*way*], going up to Jerusalem." Jesus says:

See, we are going up to Jerusalem, and the Son of Man will be handed over to the chief priests and the scribes, and they will condemn him to death; then they will hand him over to the Gentiles; they will mock him, and spit upon him, and flog him, and kill him; and after three days he will rise again. (10:32–34)

The temple authorities, here spoken of as chief priests and scribes, will hand Jesus over to the Gentiles—that is, to the imperial Roman authorities—who will kill him.

Each of these anticipations of Jesus's execution is followed by *teaching* about what it means to follow Jesus. After the first, addressed to both the disciples and the crowd, the Jesus of Mark says: "If any want to become my followers, let them deny themselves and take up their cross and follow me" (8:34). In first-century Christianity, the cross had a twofold meaning. On the one hand, it represented execution by the empire; only the empire crucified, and then for only one crime: denial of imperial authority. The cross had not yet become a generalized symbol for suffering as it sometimes is today, when one's illness or other hardship can be spoken of as "the cross I've been given to bear." Rather, it meant risking imperial retribution.

On the other hand, the cross by the time of Mark's gospel had also become a symbol for the "way" or the "path" of death and resurrection, of entering new life by dying to an old life. The cross as the "way" of transformation is found in Paul, and it is also present in Mark. Indeed, in case we might miss the point, Luke adds the word "daily" to Mark's passage about taking up the cross to make sure that that we understand that the way of the cross is the path of personal transformation (9:23).

After the second passage anticipating Jesus's execution in Jerusalem, Mark reports that Jesus asks his disciples, "What were you arguing about *on the way*?" Learning that they have been arguing about who among them was the greatest, he says, "Whoever wants to be first must be last of all and servant of all" (9:33–35). The contrast of first and last correlates with another paradoxical contrast in the teaching of Jesus: those who exalt themselves will be humbled, and those who humble themselves will be exalted. Those who puff themselves up, make something great of themselves, will be humiliated. And those who humble themselves, who make themselves empty, will be filled, exalted (Matt. 23:12). This is the way of following Jesus.

The third anticipation of Jesus execution, the longest and most detailed, is followed by the longest and most detailed exposition of what it means to follow Jesus. James and John, two of the inner circle of his followers, ask for places of honor in the kingdom they believe is coming. Jesus responds, "Are you able to drink the *cup* that I drink, or be baptized with the *baptism* that I am baptized with?" (10:38). Both cup and baptism are images of death. Later in Mark, as Jesus faces his own death, he speaks of it as his "cup" (14:36). And baptism in early Christianity was seen as a ritual enactment of dying and rising. Jesus's question means, "Are you willing to follow me on the path of death and resurrection?"

The passage continues. After the cup and baptism images, the Jesus of Mark says:

> You know that among the Gentiles those whom they recognize as their rulers lord it over them, and their great ones are tyrants over them. But it is not so among you; but whoever wishes to become great among you must be your servant, and whoever wishes to be first among you must be slave of all. (10:42–44)

The domination system—here described as being of "the Gentiles," in which "rulers lord it over them and their great ones are tyrants over them"—shall not be so among those who follow Jesus.

To underline the centrality of these chapters that speak of what it means to follow Jesus, Mark frames them with two stories of *seeing*, of blind men regaining their sight through Jesus. At the beginning, right before Peter's affirmation at Caesarea Philippi, Jesus lays his hands on a blind man in Bethsaida "and his sight was restored, and he saw everything clearly." At the end, as Jesus passes through Jericho and nears Jerusalem, Bartimaeus, a blind beggar, beseeches Jesus: "My teacher, let me see again!" Then Mark tells us, "Immediately he regained his sight *and followed Jesus on the way*" (8:22–26; 10:46–52). The framing is deliberate, the meaning clear: *to see* means to see that *the way* involves following Jesus to Jerusalem.

Thus we have the twofold theme that leads to Palm Sunday. Genuine discipleship, following Jesus, means following him to Jerusalem, the place of (1) confrontation with the domination system and (2) death and resurrection. These are the two themes of the week that follows, Holy Week. Indeed, these are the two themes of Lent and of the Christian life.

As we conclude this chapter on Sunday and the two processions that begin Holy Week, we want to guard against some possible misunderstandings of the conflict that led to Jesus's crucifixion. It was not Jesus against Judaism. Much of the scholarship of the last half century, especially the last twenty years, has rightly emphasized that we must understand Jesus within Judaism, not against Judaism. Jesus was a *part* of Judaism, not *apart* from Judaism.

The conflict is also not about priests and sacrifice, as if Jesus's primary passion was a protest against the role of priestly mediators or against animal sacrifice. Rather, his protest was against a domination system legitimated in the name of God, a domination system radically different from what the already present and coming kingdom of God, the dream of God, would be like. It was not Jesus against Judaism, or Judaism against Jesus. Rather, his was a Jewish voice, one of several first-century Jewish voices, about what loyalty to the God of Judaism meant. And for Christians, he is the decisive Jewish voice.

Two processions entered Jerusalem on that day. The same question, the same alternative, faces those who would be faithful to Jesus today. Which procession are we in? Which procession do we want to be in? This is the question of Palm Sunday and of the week that is about to unfold.

MONDAY

On the following day, when they came from Bethany, he was hungry. Seeing in the distance a fig tree in leaf, he went to see whether perhaps he would find anything on it. When he came to it, he found nothing but leaves, for it was not the season for figs. He said to it, "May no one ever eat fruit from you again." And his disciples heard it.

Then they came to Jerusalem. And he entered the temple and began to drive out those who were selling and those who were buying in the temple, and he overturned the tables of the money changers and the seats of those who sold doves; and he would not allow anyone to carry anything through the temple. He was teaching and saying, "Is it not written, 'My house shall be called a house of prayer for all the nations'? But you have made it a den of robbers." And when the chief priests and the scribes heard it, they kept looking for a way to kill him; for they were afraid of him, because the whole crowd was spellbound by his teaching.

And when evening came, Jesus and his disciples went out of the city.

MARK 11:12–19

———— •◆• ————

Imagine you had read Mark's account of Jesus's first day in Jerusalem, that day we Christians call Palm Sunday, without knowing anything about its background in Zechariah's prophecy. You might misunderstand it completely. You might think that Jesus was simply exhausted after a week's walk from Galilee and needed transportation for the last mile. Or that he wanted to be seated high enough so everyone could see him. But what we often call Jesus's triumphal entry was actually an anti-imperial, anti-triumphal one, a deliberate lampoon of the conquering emperor entering a city on horseback through gates opened in abject submission.

That is all clear enough once history and prophecy are understood. Jesus's symbolic challenge on Mark's Sunday leads into another one on Mark's Monday, and it too demands some knowledge of both history and prophecy to avoid serious misunderstanding. Indeed, to speak of Monday's "cleansing of the temple" is to misrepresent that incident just as much as to speak of Sunday's "triumphal entry" is to misinterpret the purpose of that event. Jeremiah 7 and 26 will be as significant for Mark 11:12–19 as Zechariah 9:9–10 was for Mark 11:1–11. Furthermore, as we see below, those symbolic actions form a diptych and must be held and interpreted in tandem with one another.

MARKAN FRAMES

Mark's gospel often contains pairs of incidents that are intended to be interpreted in light of one another. In the narrative sequence they vibrate together, each reflecting meaning upon the other. That is done by an intercalation, or framing technique, in which *Incident A* begins, then *Incident B* begins, continues, concludes, and finally *Incident A* continues and concludes. In this book we call them *frames*. Here are a few examples:

Incident A¹:	3:20–21	5:21–24	6:7–13	11:12–14	14:1–2	14:53–54
Incident B:	3:22–30	5:25–34	6:14–29	11:15–19	14:3–9	14:55–65
Incident A²:	3:31–35	5:35–43	6:30	11:20–21	14:10–11	14:66–72

Each of those cases challenged first-century hearers and also challenges twenty-first century readers to probe for understanding. How exactly do the framing *Incident A* and the framed *Incident B* shed light on one another?

Take, for example, that first sequence in Mark 3:20–35. *Incident A* concerns Jesus and his family. It starts in the first, or *A¹*, frame in 3:20–21 with this: "The crowd came together again, so that they could not even eat. When his family [members] heard it, they went out to restrain him, for people [literally, they] were saying, 'He has gone out of his mind.'" There is no mention of "people" in Greek—it is simply the third-person plural pronoun "they," and in context that means the "family [members]," which is plural in Greek. In other words, Jesus's birth-family members are rejecting him as insane. No wonder, by the way, that our English translation mutes that rejection and changes "family" to "people."

The opening frame of *Incident A¹* then stops, and *Incident B* takes over the story in 3:22 with, "The scribes who came down from Jerusalem said, 'He has Beelzebul, and by the ruler of the demons he casts out demons.'" Jesus rebuts the accusation as illogical in 3:26: "If Satan has risen up against himself and is divided, he cannot stand, but his end has come." But he also notes: "If a kingdom is divided against itself, that kingdom cannot stand. And if a house is divided against itself, that house will not be able to stand" (3:24–25). That rebuttal points in two directions at once: toward the framed "kingdom," or domain, of Satan and toward the framing "house," or family, of Jesus. In other words, when Jesus makes the indictment that "whoever blasphemes against the Holy Spirit can never have forgiveness, but is guilty of an eternal sin" (3:29), it is directed against both the family from Nazareth and the scribes from Jerusalem.

By that stage we are somewhat prepared for the closing *Incident A²* concerning Jesus's family in 3:31–35, which picks up where 3:20–21 went on hold. There Jesus replaces, as it were, his blood family with a faith family. When the "crowd was sitting around him; and they said to him, 'Your mother and your brothers and sisters are outside, asking for you,'" Jesus responds by "looking at those who sat around him" and saying, "Whoever does the will of God is my brother and sister and mother."

Mark describes as blasphemy against the Holy Spirit *both* the familial accusation of madness and the scribal accusation of possession. Both allegations place Jesus's mission and message, life and program under alien forces and out from under divine control, and Jesus rejects that notion. Mark's framing technique pushes hearers or readers to meditate deeply on the intercalation of those two dismissals by Jesus. Think, it says, and keep on thinking. So now, with that literary-theological technique in 3:20–35 as example, we turn to the first of three cases from Mark's last week of Jesus.

FROM THE FIG TREE LEARN ITS LESSON

Mark begins the Monday of Jesus's last week in 11:12–14. Jesus and the disciples are coming from Bethany to Jerusalem. Hungry, Jesus sees a fig tree and, not finding any figs on it, pronounces a curse that it would never produce figs again, a curse the disciples hear. Next follows the incident in 11:15–19, which is usually misnamed as the "cleansing of the temple" and sometimes cutely dismissed as "Jesus's temple tantrum." Finally, on Tuesday, Mark concludes in 11:20–21 with: "In the morning as they passed by, they saw the fig tree withered away to its roots. Then Peter remembered and said to him, 'Rabbi, look! The fig tree that you cursed has withered.'" That passage, of course, is a typical Markan frame:

Incident A¹: The fig tree is cursed,
             and the disciples hear.   11:12–14
Incident B: The incident in the temple.   11:15–19
Incident A²: The fig tree is withered,
             and Peter remembers.   11:20–21

Mark, in other words, wants hearers or readers to consider those two incidents together, so that what happened to the fig tree and what happened in the temple interpret each other.

Mark emphasizes two somewhat contradictory points about the fig tree. On the one hand, it was Passover week, the month was Nisan, or March-April to us, and there could never have been figs on that tree. Anyone and everyone would have known that, in Mark's words, "it was not the season for figs." On the other hand, according to Mark, Jesus was hungry, expected to find figs, and, having failed to do so, cursed the tree to permanent barrenness.

The obvious contradiction between those two aspects of the incident is Mark's way of warning us to take the event symbolically rather than historically. Taken factually, Jesus is unreasonably petulant, if not petulantly abusive, of his divine power. But taken as a parable, the fig tree's failure is a cipher for that of the temple. The framing fig tree warns us that the framed temple is not being cleansed, but symbolically destroyed and that, in both cases, the problem is a lack of the "fruit" that Jesus expected to be present. But what exactly was wrong with the temple? Was Jesus's expectation for the temple every bit as strange as that for the fig tree? Was Jesus's action in the temple every bit as strange as that with the fig tree?

Before continuing with Mark's story, we pause to clear up some misunderstandings about the context of the temple incident. All too often in the past, we Christians have misread the action of Jesus in the temple at Jerusalem and allowed much later debates to infiltrate its original meaning. Debates, often more bitter than accurate, between Christians and Jews and disputes, again more bitter than accurate, between Catholic and Protestant Christians have misinterpreted Jesus's temple action as a statement against sacrifice or the priesthood or even the temple itself. Maybe Jesus was attacking the institution of *blood sacrifices*—since no Christians practice that any longer—or even attacking *sacrifice* as such—since some Christians avoid that very concept? Maybe Jesus was opposing the institution of *priesthood*—since some Christians have no priests? Maybe Jesus's action repudiated the *temple itself,* representing Christianity repudiating Judaism?

Against that background of potential anti-Judaism or even anti-Semitism, it is necessary first to look at first-century Judaism's blood sacrifice, high-priesthood, and temple ritual. Only then will we be ready to understand Jesus's action in the temple according to Mark 11:15–19.

THE MEANING OF BLOOD SACRIFICE

We focus on animal blood sacrifice because that form of worship is most outside our general experience and may be the one most likely to lead to a misunderstanding of Jesus's action in Jerusalem's temple. For those who are vegetarians for moral reasons, the slaughter of animals for food is ethically repugnant. Animal blood sacrifice would be repugnant to them as well. But most people in the ancient world took blood sacrifice for granted as a normal or even supreme form of religious piety. Why?

First, the vast majority of people in antiquity grew up in close contact with animals on land they either owned themselves or farmed for others, and most of them would have killed animals for food or at least seen it happen. In any case, the ancients knew that to eat meat or have a feast, you had first to kill an animal. We know that too of course, and in fact we eat far more meat than they ever did, but few of us have seen our meat killed and butchered before it is offered to us as food. We get our meat plastic-wrapped at the supermarket, and many of us could not watch the bloody process by which it got from field to store.

Second, and long before animal sacrifice was invented, human beings knew two rather basic ways of creating, maintaining, or restoring good relations with one another—the gift and the meal. Each represents the external manifestation of an internal disposition. Each has its own delicate protocols of what, when, why, to whom, and by whom. The proffered gift and the shared meal are probably the most ancient forms of human interaction, possibly even more fundamental than sex as a bonding activity.

How, then, did people create, maintain, or restore good relations with a divine being? What visible acts could they do to reach an Invisible Being? Again, they could give a gift or share a meal. In sacrifice *as gift*, an offerer took a valuable animal or other foodstuff and gave it to God by having it burned on the altar. In this case, the animal was totally destroyed at least as far as the offerer was concerned. No doubt the smoke and smell rising upward symbolized the transition of the gift from earth to heaven, from human being to God. In sacrifice *as meal*, the animal was transferred to God by having its blood poured over the altar and was then returned to the offerer as divine food for a feast with God. In other words, the offerer did not so much invite God to a meal as God invited the offerer to a meal.

That understanding of sacrifice clarifies the etymology of the term. It derives from the Latin *sacrum facere*, "to make" (*facere*) "sacred" (*sacrum*). In a sacrifice the animal is *made sacred* and is given to God as a sacred gift or returned to the offerer as a sacred meal. That sense of *sacrifice* should never be confused with either *suffering* or *substitution*.

First, sacrifice and suffering. Offerers never thought that the point of sacrifice was to make the animal suffer, or that the greatest sacrifice was one in which the animal suffered lengthily and terribly. For a human meal or a divine meal an animal had to be slain, but that was done swiftly and efficiently—ancient priests were also excellent butchers.

Second, sacrifice and substitution. Offerers never thought that the animal was dying in their place, that they deserved to be killed in punishment for their sins, but that God would accept the slain animal as substitutionary atonement or vicarious satisfaction. Blood sacrifice should never be confused with or collapsed into either suffering or substitution, let alone substitutionary suffering. We may or may not like ancient blood sacrifice, but we should neither caricature nor libel it.

As an aside, think about our ordinary use of that term "sacrifice" even today. A building is on fire and a child is trapped upstairs; a firefighter rushes in to get him and manages to drop him safely to the net below before the roof caves in and kills her. The next day the local paper headlines "Firefighter Sacrifices Her Life." We are not ancients, but moderns, and yet that is still an absolutely acceptable statement. On the one hand, all human life and all human death are sacred. On the other, that firefighter has *made* her own death peculiarly, especially, emphatically *sacred* by giving it up to save the life of another. So far, so good. Now imagine if somebody confused sacrifice with suffering and denied it was a sacrifice because the firefighter died instantly and without intolerable suffering. Or imagine if somebody confused sacrifice with substitution, saying that God wanted somebody dead that day and accepted the firefighter in lieu of the child. And worst of all, imagine that somebody brought together sacrifice, suffering, and substitution by claiming that the firefighter had to die in agony as atonement for the sins of the child's parents. That theology would be a crime against divinity.

Back, then, to ancient blood sacrifice as gift or meal, but not as suffering or substitution. Like the rest of their world, most Jews accepted blood sacrifice as a normal and normative component of divine worship at the time of Jesus. There is no reason to think that Jesus's action in the temple was caused by any rejection of blood sacrifice or, indeed, had anything to do with sacrifice as such. There were other powerful forces of ambiguity at play in first-century Israel with regard, first, to the official high-priesthood and, through its members, even to the temple itself.

THE AMBIGUITY OF THE HIGH-PRIESTHOOD

Today some Christian denominations have priests and some do not, but post-Reformation tensions over the clergy either as function or caste should not be retrojected into Jesus's temple action. Instead, we focus on the relationship between the high priest Caiaphas and the governor Pilate as an instance of the ambiguous status of the high-priesthood itself at the time of Jesus.

In the century of independence that ended in 63 BCE, the Jewish Hasmonean or Maccabean leaders had, through successful wars against Syrian imperialism, elevated their status to that of high priests and kings to become priest-kings. That usurpation of the hereditary high-priesthood may well have led the more legitimate high-priestly family and its followers to withdraw to Qumran, where the Dead Sea Scrolls were discovered around the middle of the last century. That is probably why that group, whom we name the Essenes, expected two separate messiahs, one priestly and one royal, rather than just one (and the priestly messiah took precedence over the royal one). Obviously the Qumran community was not against priests or high priests as such, but only against those contemporary ones they deemed invalid. And the high-priesthood would not have been viewed any more favorably by those dissidents when the Herodians and then the Romans took over Judea, hiring and firing high priests at will. The high-priesthood had become ambiguous at best.

Over half a millennium afterward, the Babylonian Talmud recalls a poetic indictment from the first century that accuses the four main high-priestly families of violence against the ordinary people:

Woe is me because of the House of Beothus,
woe is me because of the staves.
Woe is me because of the House of Hanan,
woe is me because of their whisperings.

Woe is me because of the House of Kathros,
woe is me because of their pens.
Woe is me because of the House of Ishmael, son of Phiabi,
woe is me because of their fists.
For they are the high priests,
and their sons are treasurers,
and their sons-in-law are trustees,
and their servants beat the people with staves. (*Pesahim* 57)

As you probably noticed, the word "staves"—we would say "clubs"—frames that fourfold accusation's beginning and ending. But what exactly was the problem behind that sweeping dismissal?

Of the four high-priestly families indicted by those multiplied "woes" above, that of Hanan (same as Annas, Ananus, or Ananias) was the most powerful prior to the war of 66–74 CE. That family had eight high priests who ruled cumulatively for almost forty years. Hanan I ruled 6–15 CE, and after him there were five sons, one son-in-law, and one grandson as high priests. It also seems that Jesus and all those first-century Christian Jews whose deaths we know about in the Jewish homeland were executed under high priests from the family of Hanan: Stephen in Acts 6–7; James, the brother of John, in Acts 12; and James, the brother of Jesus in Josephus's *Jewish Antiquities* 20.197–203.

In any imperial situation the foreign power must operate with local and indigenous cooperation. That would be true of any Roman governor anywhere and, as an aristocrat himself, he would expect to collaborate with the local aristocracy. But Judea was a special case. Pilate, as governor, was subject to the ultimate authority of the Syrian legate, and he was operating in a temple state. In ordinary Roman society any aristocrat could be a priest, but in Judea the high priests were drawn from a few special families. There was no longer a single hereditary dynasty that established the next high priest for life; instead, there were those four major families competing with one another for that supreme office. And the governor could hire and fire the high priest and could use those families in the classical imperial mode of divide and conquer.

That administrative situation was bad for all concerned. How could a high priest negotiate with a governor who could fire him? In terms of imperial rule, a governor looking over his shoulder at a legate and a high priest looking over his shoulder at a governor is a recipe for misrule. But Caiaphas, son-in-law of Annas, was high priest from 18 to 36 CE, eighteen years in a century when four years was about average. Pilate was Roman governor of Judea from 26 to 36 CE. We must presume that the Romans and Caiaphas worked well together. It is not necessary to demonize either Caiaphas or Pilate, but it would seem that, even from the viewpoint of Roman imperial rule, they collaborated not wisely but too well. When Pilate was recalled to Rome, Caiaphas was deposed and Jonathan appointed in his place.

Finally, after the war broke out against the Romans in 66 CE and their best general, Vespasian, was storming southward and forcing peasant insurgent bands into the doomed city of Jerusalem, one of the first actions of those "Zealots" was to attack the reigning aristocratic high priest as illegitimate and appoint a legitimate peasant one by lot.

It was, in other words, quite possible in first-century Judea to deny the very validity of the ruling high-priesthood or to be against high-priestly competition and collaboration without that involving any negation of the Jewish priesthood in general or even of the high-priesthood in particular. It was possible to be against a particular high priest and the manner in which he was fulfilling his role without being against the office of high priest itself. There was a terrible ambiguity in that the priest who represented the Jews before God on the Day of Atonement also represented them before Rome the rest of the year.

THE AMBIGUITY OF THE TEMPLE

That ambiguity of Judaism's high priest as Rome's primary local collaborator spilled over to the temple as well. That building was both the house of God on earth and the institutional seat of submission to Rome.

On the one hand, there is not the slightest doubt that Jews from all over the Mediterranean world looked to their homeland and its great temple with affection and pride and supported it through taxation and pilgrimage. Every male over a certain age showed that loyalty by freely paying an annual temple tax of a half-shekel, or two denarii, per year (think of one denarius as a day's pay for a laborer). And all of those small donations added up to a very large amount. For example, in Apamea, just one city of Asia Minor, Cicero tells us that the amount collected was almost a hundred pounds of gold.

Moreover, Jews were willing to die for the integrity of their temple. In 40–41 CE, when the emperor Caligula planned to install in the temple a statue of himself as Zeus incarnate, "tens of thousands" of unarmed homeland Jews were ready to die as non-violent martyrs to prevent that terrible blasphemy against their holy temple. According to both the Jewish philosopher Philo in his *Embassy to Gaius* (22–49) and the Jewish historian Josephus in both his *Jewish War* (2.192–97) and *Jewish Antiquities* (18.263–72), huge groups of "men, women, and children" confronted the Syrian legate Petronius at Ptolemais and Tiberias as he moved southward with the statue and two legions to enforce its installation in the temple. Thousands of unarmed martyrs would have died to protect the holiness of their temple.

On the other hand, after Herod had massively rebuilt the platform of the temple and added a giant Court of the Gentiles—which, by the way, created no resistance that we know about—he placed a large golden eagle, symbol of Rome and its supreme divinity, Jupiter Optimus Maximus, atop one of its gates. Most likely, that gate was at the end of the western access bridge from the Upper City and the homes of the high-priestly families. It may have been necessary to reassure Caesar Augustus that such a gigantic edifice was a pro-Roman temple and not an anti-Roman fortress. In any case, two Jewish teachers told their students to hack it off the wall since it was contrary to their sacred laws.

What happened? This, according to Josephus's accounts in both *Jewish War* (1.648–55) and *Jewish Antiquities* (17.149–67): "The king's captain ... with a considerable force, arrested about forty of the young men and conducted them to the king.... Those who had let themselves down from the roof together with the doctors he had burnt alive; the remainder of those arrested he handed over to his executioners." Those martyrs had not, of course, acted against the temple, but against the ambiguity of the Roman eagle on the Jewish temple. Was the temple the house of Yahweh or of Jupiter?

Once again, that ambiguity meant that faithful Jews could be very much against the temple as it was at that time without in any way being against the theory or practice of the temple and the existence of priests and high priests, let alone the normalcy of animal blood sacrifices. We only emphasize those elements to keep Christian experience, which does *not* include them, from infiltrating and distorting our understanding of what Jesus did in the temple.

The temple's ambiguity was, however, far more ancient than any problem with Caiaphas's collusion with Pilate in particular or high-priestly collaboration with Rome in general. It goes back over half a millennium, back, for example, to the time of the prophet Jeremiah, one of the major prophets of the Jewish Bible, who spoke to Jerusalem for several decades around 600 BCE.

JEREMIAH AND THE TEMPLE

In Jeremiah 7 God tells Jeremiah to stand in front of the temple and confront those who enter to worship (7:1). About what? About their false sense of security. Their clinging to the refrain "This is the temple of the Lord, the temple of the Lord, the temple of the Lord" (7:4) indicates that they are taking it for granted that God's presence in the temple guarantees the security of Jerusalem and their own security as well. Do you think, charges God through Jeremiah, that divine worship excuses you from divine justice, that all God wants is regular attendance at God's temple rather than equitable distribution of God's land? Here is the *accusation:*

> If you truly amend your ways and your doings, if you truly act justly one with another, if you do not oppress the alien, the orphan, and the widow, or shed innocent blood in this place, and if you do not go after other gods to your own hurt, then I will dwell with you in this place, in the land that I gave of old to your ancestors forever and ever. . . . Has this house, which is called by my name, become a den of robbers in your sight? (7:5–7, 11)

In that context the meaning of the phrase "den of robbers" is very clear. The people's everyday injustice makes them robbers, and they think the temple is their safe house, den, hideaway, or place of security. The temple is not the place where the robbery occurs, but the place the robbers go for refuge.

Jeremiah, of course, is not inventing anything new with that indictment. There was an ancient prophetic *tradition* in which God insisted not just on justice *and* worship, but on justice *over* worship. God had repeatedly said, "I reject your worship because of your lack of justice," but never, ever, ever, "I reject your justice because of your lack of worship." Here is a medley of passages:

> I hate, I despise your festivals, and I take no delight in your solemn assemblies. Even though you offer me your burnt offerings and grain offerings, I will not accept them; and the offerings of well-being of your fatted animals I will not look

upon. Take away from me the noise of your songs; I will not
listen to the melody of your harps. But let justice roll down
like waters, and righteousness like an ever-flowing stream.
(Amos 5:21–24)

I desire steadfast love and not sacrifice, the knowledge of
God rather than burnt offerings. (Hos. 6:6)

With what shall I come before the Lord, and bow myself
before God on high? Shall I come before him with burnt
offerings, with calves a year old? Will the Lord be pleased
with thousands of rams, with ten thousands of rivers of oil?
Shall I give my firstborn for my transgression, the fruit of
my body for the sin of my soul? He has told you, O mortal,
what is good; and what does the Lord require of you but to
do justice, and to love kindness, and to walk humbly with
your God? (Mic. 6:6–8)

What to me is the multitude of your sacrifices? says the
Lord; I have had enough of burnt offerings of rams and the
fat of fed beasts; I do not delight in the blood of bulls, or of
lambs, or of goats. When you come to appear before me, who
asked this from your hand? Trample my courts no more;
bringing offerings is futile; incense is an abomination to me.
New moon and sabbath and calling of convocation—I cannot endure solemn assemblies with iniquity. Your new moons
and your appointed festivals my soul hates; they have become
a burden to me, I am weary of bearing them. When you
stretch out your hands, I will hide my eyes from you; even
though you make many prayers, I will not listen; your hands
are full of blood. Wash yourselves; make yourselves clean; remove the evil of your doings from before my eyes; cease to do
evil, learn to do good; seek justice, rescue the oppressed, defend the orphan, plead for the widow. (Isa. 1:11–17)

Since God is just and the world belongs to God, worship cannot be separated from justice because worship or union with a God of justice empowers the worshipper for a life of justice. Back now to Jeremiah 7.

Next, Jeremiah utters a terrible *threat* in the name of God. What will happen if worship in the house of God continues as a substitute for justice in the land of God? This is what will happen:

> Go now to my place that was in Shiloh, where I made my name dwell at first, and see what I did to it for the wickedness of my people Israel. And now, because you have done all these things, says the Lord, and when I spoke to you persistently, you did not listen, and when I called you, you did not answer, therefore I will do to the house that is called by my name, in which you trust, and to the place that I gave to you and to your ancestors, just what I did to Shiloh. (7:12–14)

Shiloh, which was later destroyed by the Philistines, was the place where the ark of the covenant was enshrined in the tent of God before it was removed to the temple of God built by Solomon. The threat is clear: if God's temple is used as a place where worship is substituted for justice, God will destroy that temple, since it has become a haven for perpetrators of injustice and a den for robbers.

What happens to Jeremiah after he pronounces that threat from God? Nothing in Jeremiah 7, but a lot in a twin version of the text in Jeremiah 26. There the *accusation* explicitly refers to the preceding prophetic *tradition* and concludes with the same *threat*. If the people do not turn from "evil" and do not "heed the words of ... the prophets," then God will destroy this temple "like Shiloh" (26:1–6). But now comes a very new element. There is a furious *reaction* that almost costs Jeremiah his life—how dare he say that God might destroy God's own house?

At first *both the authorities and the people* are against Jeremiah and declare that he "deserves the sentence of death because he has prophesied against this city, as you have heard with your own ears" (26:11) but eventually "the officials and all the people said to the priests and the prophets, 'This man does not deserve the sentence of death, for he has spoken to us in the name of the Lord our God'" (26:16). And so, finally, Jeremiah "was not given over into the hands of the people to be put to death" (26:24). Hold that agreement of *authorities and people*—be it to execute or not to execute Jeremiah—in your mind as we return again to Jesus's deed-and-word in the Temple.

JESUS AND THE DEN OF ROBBERS

The Temple incident involved both an *action* by Jesus and a *teaching* that accompanied and presumably explained it. That combination is typical for prophetic symbols. In the 590s BCE, for example, the prophets Jeremiah and Hananiah perform opposing symbolic actions in the context of the rising power of the Babylonian empire. The question is whether Judea should or should not submit to its power.

Jeremiah put a yoke of straps and bars on his neck and advised submission to the Babylonians—in the name of God: "Serve the king of Babylon and live. Why should this city become a desolation?" (27:2, 17). But Hananiah took and broke the yoke from Jeremiah's neck and advises rebellion—in the name of God: "I will break the yoke of King Nebuchadnezzar of Babylon from the neck of all the nations within two years" (28:10-11). In prophetic and symbolic saying-and-acting combinations, deed-and-word should be used to interpret each other.

So also with Jesus's deed and word in the temple. Here is the full text in Mark:

> Then they came to Jerusalem. And he entered the temple and began to drive out those who were selling and those who were buying in the temple, and he overturned the tables

of the money changers and the seats of those who sold doves; and he would not allow anyone to carry anything through the temple. He was teaching and saying, "Is it not written, 'My house shall be called a house of prayer for all the nations'? But you have made it a den of robbers." And when the chief priests and the scribes heard it, they kept looking for a way to kill him; for they were afraid of him, because the whole crowd was spellbound by his teaching. (11:15–18)

And, for future reference, notice that contrasting reaction, lethal from the "chief priests and the scribes" but very supportive from "the whole crowd."

First, the *action*. Four parts to the action are mentioned in Mark 11:15–16. Jesus (1) began to drive out the buyers and the sellers, (2) overturned the tables of the money changers, (3) overturned the seats of the dove sellers, and (4) would not allow anyone to carry anything through the temple. We emphasize that the money changers and animal sellers were perfectly legitimate and absolutely necessary for the temple's normal functioning. The buying and selling all took place in the huge Court of the Gentiles. Money changers were needed so that Jewish pilgrims could pay the temple tax in the only approved coinage. Buying animals or birds on site was the only way pilgrims could be sure the creatures were ritually adequate for sacrifice.

What does it mean that Jesus has interrupted the temple's perfectly legitimate sacrificial and fiscal activities? It means that Jesus has *shut down the temple*. But it is a symbolic rather than a literal "shutdown." It is a prophetic action that intends in macrocosm what it effects in microcosm. It is the same as pouring blood on draft files in one single office during the Vietnam War. The Pentagon is not "shut down" literally, but it is "shut down" symbolically. At this point, the Markan frames of fig tree and temple coalesce. The tree was "shut down" for lack of the fruit Jesus demanded—and so also was the temple. In the case of the temple, it is not a cleansing, but a symbolic destruction, and the fig tree's fate emphasizes that meaning. But what is wrong with the temple to warrant such a symbolic destruction? The answer must come from the *word* that follows the *deed* in this prophetic action.

Second, the *saying*. It is recorded in Mark 11:17: "He was teaching and saying, 'Is it not written, "My house shall be called a house of prayer for all the nations"? But you have made it a den of robbers.'" One tiny point about Jesus's biblical citations before continuing. Gospel footnotes usually indicate the sources as Isaiah 56:7 (for the "house of prayer" part) and Jeremiah 7:11 (for the "den of robbers" part), but the former is given in quotation marks, and the latter is not. In other words, that "den of robbers" is not indicated clearly as a quotation, and that has played heavily into Christian misunderstandings of Jesus's action. Without going back to the scriptural context for that phrase, "den" is ignored and "robbery" taken to refer to what is going on in the outer Court of the Gentiles—the changing of money and the selling of animals. But clearly from the quotation's context in Jeremiah 7 and 26, a "den" is a hideaway, a safe house, a refuge. It is not where robbers rob, but where they flee for safety after having done their robbing elsewhere.

As Mark explains with his fig-tree frames and as Jesus's citation of Jeremiah emphasizes, the prophetic action is a destruction of the temple, a symbolic "shutdown" in fulfillment of God's threat in Jeremiah 7 and 26. There is nothing wrong with prayer and sacrifice—they are commanded in Torah. That is not the problem. But God is a God of justice and righteousness and when worship substitutes for justice, God rejects God's temple— or, for us today, God's church.

FOR ALL THE NATIONS

What about Jesus's first quotation, from Isaiah 56:7, which precedes the "den of robbers" one just seen from Jeremiah 7:11: "My house shall be called a house of prayer for all the nations"? It is necessary at this point to make a distinction between what Jesus said and what Mark added to it here.

On the one hand, it is difficult to imagine the historical Jesus using that quotation from Isaiah. Why? Because of where he was standing.

Herod the Great undertook two of the greatest construction projects of his time, and he did them simultaneously. One was a huge all-weather port on Judea's Mediterranean coast at Caesarea Maritima. The other and very much connected project was the new platform for the temple in Jerusalem, an extension that cut into the northern mount and built up the southern slope until the overall platform was five football fields long and three wide. And most of that was the new Court of the Gentiles, separated to be sure from that of the Jews, but taking up the vast majority of the temple's space through which all those Jews had to pass. Herod's temple was now a sacred microcosm of God's world—at its center was the Holy of Holies; around that were the courtyards of Jewish priests, followed by those of Jewish males and then those of Jewish females, and finally the huge courtyard of the Gentiles.

In the year 30 CE, therefore, neither Jesus nor anyone else could stand where the money changers sat and the pure animals were sold and say that the temple was not open to all people, that it was not "a house of prayer for all the nations [*ethnē* in Greek]." They could not say that in any case, but certainly not while standing in the Court of the Gentiles (*ethnē* in Greek).

On the other, it is very easy to see why Mark would have added a quotation from Isaiah to an original Jesus quotation of Jeremiah. He is thinking not so much of Jesus around 30 CE as of his own people forty years later. They have gone through the agonies of the great rebellion against Rome in 66–74, and Mark is writing sometime after the destruction of Jerusalem and its temple in 70. He is explaining to Christian Jews who survived that tragedy why God allowed it to happen, and his interpretation is remarkably similar to that of Josephus. We shall see this same interpretation later when Mark speaks about Barabbas and mentions those crucified along with Jesus.

One linguistic point before we continue. The word translated in the Greek of Jeremiah 7:11 and Mark 11:17 as "robber" is actually *lēstēs,* and that term more properly means "bandit," "brigand," "rebel," or any form of armed resistance to established control. It could, of course, include large-scale robbery (but not small-time thievery), since that was a calculated refusal of normal law and order. For some Jews under imperial control, *lēstēs* might designate a freedom fighter, but for all Romans it meant an insurgent. In general, then, it meant any form of violent resistance to Roman control that was neither territorial rebellion nor standard warfare.

Back now to Josephus and Mark, who are both speaking about the temple's destruction in the year 70 CE. First, Josephus. Recall, as mentioned earlier, those peasant partisans, rebel group, or "Zealots" swept into Jerusalem by the Roman advance between 67 and 70. Josephus detested those lower-class rebels because they enacted a French Revolution–style reign of terror against their own lay and priestly aristocracy even as all were preparing (or not preparing!) for a Roman legionary siege. Josephus' specific term for them is the "Zealots," but his more general term is that just-seen Greek word *lēstēs.* In other words, Josephus could easily have described that Zealot-controlled temple as a den of robbers or hideout of brigands. But of course it was not their social injustice outside the temple, but their civil war inside it that appalled Josephus.

Turn now to Mark and our suggestion that he has inserted that citation of Isaiah 56:7 ("house of prayer") before the pre-Markan one from Jeremiah 7:11 ("den of robbers"). Jesus could not have denied that Herod's great Court of the Gentiles was "a house of prayer for all the nations" in the year 30 CE, but Mark could certainly do so around the year 70. Between 67 and 70 the temple

was certainly no longer open to "all the nations," but had become
a stronghold for Zealot insurgents, a stronghold initially against
their own Jewish aristocracy and eventually against the besieg-
ing Roman legions. Our conclusion, therefore, is that the pre-
Markan combination of symbolic action as fulfillment of the
prophetic citation from Jeremiah goes back to the historical Jesus
himself. Jesus's action in the temple was a symbolic fulfillment of
Jeremiah's prophetic threat about its divine destruction if worship
substituted for justice.

TWIN SYMBOLIC ACTIONS

As Mark outlines Jesus's last week, each of the two opening days
contains a radical symbolic action accompanied by an earlier
prophetic citation. The Sunday demonstration occurs at the entrance to Jerusalem, the Monday one at the entrance to the
temple. But for Mark those are not so much two separate incidents as a single double one. And he emphasizes that parallelism
in three ways.

First of all, there is the general structure of Sunday and Monday with these three major elements:

	Entrance Demonstration	*Temple Demonstration*
1. Arrival at Jerusalem	11:1a	11:15a
2. Prophetic action	11:1b–10	11:15b–17
3. Departure from Jerusalem	11:11b	11:19

Second, there is that pivotal verse in 11:11 at the end of Sunday's
entrance demonstration that prepares for and connects to Monday's temple demonstration: "Then he entered Jerusalem and went
into the temple; and when he had looked around at everything, as
it was already late, he went out to Bethany with the twelve."

Third, that verse also serves to emphasize that, just as the entrance demonstration was a preplanned one, so also was that temple one a preplanned action. Mornings not evenings, after all, are the best time for major demonstrations. Matthew, by the way, found Mark 11:11 so strange that his own temple incident takes place the same Sunday evening as Jesus's first arrival at the temple (21:12).

Mark considers each event a preplanned demonstration of prophetic criticism and, furthermore, considers them preplanned as tandem incidents. And, in case it is still necessary after so many past misunderstandings, we insist once again that neither of those symbolic actions was an attack on Judaism as a religion, on the priesthood or even the high-priesthood as an institution, or on the temple as a location for blood sacrifice.

We now turn from what Jesus's symbolic actions do not mean to what they do mean. Taken together, and they must be taken together, those action-word combinations proclaim the *already present* kingdom of God against both the *already present* Roman imperial power and the *already present* Jewish high-priestly collaboration. Jerusalem had to be retaken by a nonviolent messiah rather than by a violent revolution, and the temple ritual had to empower justice rather than excuse one from it. What is involved for Jesus is an absolute criticism not only of violent domination, but of any religious collaboration with it. In that criticism, of course, he stands *with* the prophets of Israel such as Zechariah for the anti-imperial entry against violence and Jeremiah for the anti-temple action against injustice, but he also stands *against* those forms of Christianity that were used throughout the centuries to support imperial violence and injustice.

THREE

TUESDAY

In the morning as they passed by, they saw the fig tree withered away to its roots. Then Peter remembered and said to him, "Rabbi, look! The fig tree that you cursed has withered." Jesus answered them, "Have faith in God. Truly I tell you, if you say to this mountain, 'Be taken up and thrown into the sea,' and if you do not doubt in your heart, but believe that what you say will come to pass, it will be done for you. So I tell you, whatever you ask for in prayer, believe that you have received it, and it will be yours.

"Whenever you stand praying, forgive, if you have anything against anyone; so that your Father in heaven may also forgive you your trespasses."

MARK 11:20-25

Tuesday is a busy day, a full day. Mark's narrative of the day's events covers almost three chapters, 11:27–13:37, a total of 115 verses. The next longest days are Thursday (60 verses) and Friday (47 verses). Tuesday is thus the longest day in Mark's story of Jesus's final week.

About two-thirds of Tuesday consists of conflict with temple authorities and their associates. The remaining third (chap. 13) warns of the destruction of Jerusalem and the temple and speaks of the coming of the Son of Man, all in the near future.

The day begins with a flashback to Monday by closing the frame of the fig tree around the temple incident. Tuesday morning, as Jesus and his followers return to Jerusalem from nearby Bethany, where they had spent the night, they see the fig tree "withered away to its roots." The fig tree symbolizes Jerusalem and the temple: Mark juxtaposes the withered fig tree with a saying about "this mountain"—that is, Mt. Zion, on which the temple stood—being "thrown into the sea." In closing, as in opening, the fig tree frames and reflects on Jesus's deed and word in the temple.

As Tuesday continues, Jesus and his followers arrive in Jerusalem and enter the "temple," not meaning the sanctuary itself (which was quite small), but the large open-air courts and porticoes of the temple platform. This area was often the scene of teaching, and during Passover week it was thronged with pilgrims. All of Mark 11:25–12:44 happens in this very public setting.

The authorities and their associates challenge Jesus with a series of questions intended to entrap and discredit him in the presence of the crowd. Jesus responds in an equally challenging way, sometimes turning the questions back upon them, sometimes directly indicting them. To use technical scholarly language, these are "challenge and riposte" stories.

JESUS'S AUTHORITY IS CHALLENGED

Again they came to Jerusalem. As he was walking in the temple, the chief priests, the scribes, and the elders came to him and said, "By what authority are you doing these things? Who gave you this authority to do them?" Jesus said to them, "I will ask you one question; answer me, and I will tell you by what authority I do these things. Did the baptism of John come from heaven, or was it of human origin? Answer me." They argued with one another, "If we say, 'From heaven,' he will say, 'Why then did you not believe him?' But shall we say, 'Of human origin'?"—they were afraid of the crowd, for all regarded John as truly a prophet. So they answered Jesus, "We do not know." And Jesus said to them, "Neither will I tell you by what authority I am doing these things."

MARK 11:27–33

——— ◆ ———

As Jesus enters the temple area, the authorities immediately question him about his authority in 11:27–33. Mark names the interrogators as "the chief priests, the elders, and the scribes." The first two groups were at the top of the local system of collaboration and domination, and the scribes were a literate class employed by them.

They ask Jesus, "By what authority are you doing these things?" The question refers to Jesus's prophetic act in the temple on Monday, and Mark's use of the plural "things" suggests that Sunday's provocative entry into the city may also be included. The question is intended to lure Jesus into making a claim that might incriminate him.

Jesus parries the question by offering to answer it if they will first answer one of his. Then he asks them a question about his mentor John the Baptizer. Did the authority for his baptism "come from heaven"? That is, was it from God or was it "of human origin"? The question puts the authorities on the defensive. They confer among themselves. Either response would have discredited them. The first would have opened them up to the charge of hypocrisy. The second risked turning the crowd against them. Indeed, as Mark tells us, "They were afraid of the crowd."

Not liking either option, they say, "We do not know." At best, it is an awkward response. We may imagine chagrin and clenched teeth. Then, keeping his end of the bargain, Jesus refuses to answer their question. He has not only evaded their trap, but made them look foolish. It is brilliant.

JESUS INDICTS THE AUTHORITIES
WITH A PARABLE

Then he began to speak to them in parables. "A man planted a vineyard, put a fence around it, dug a pit for the wine press, and built a watchtower; then he leased it to tenants and went to another country. When the season came, he sent a slave to the tenants to collect from them his share of the produce of the vineyard. But they seized him, and beat him, and sent him away empty-handed. And again he sent another slave to them; this one they beat over the head and insulted. Then he sent another, and that one they killed. And so it was with many others; some they beat, and others they killed. He had still one other, a beloved son. Finally he sent him to them, saying, 'They will respect my son.' But those tenants said to one another, 'This is the heir; come, let us kill him, and the inheritance will be ours.' So they seized him, killed him, and threw him out of the vineyard. What then will the owner of the vineyard do? He will come and destroy the tenants and give the vineyard to others. Have you not read this scripture: 'The stone that the builders rejected has become the cornerstone; this was the Lord's doing, and it is amazing in our eyes'?"

When they realized that he had told this parable against them, they wanted to arrest him, but they feared the crowd. So they left him and went away.

MARK 12:1–12

———◆———

Now Jesus takes the initiative in 12:1–12. At the beginning, Jesus tells a parable about a vineyard. The story is familiar: with great care, a man plants a vineyard, puts a fence around it, digs a pit for the wine press, erects a watchtower, and then leases it to tenants. When the owner sends a servant to collect his share of the produce, the tenants beat him and send him away with nothing. The owner sends several more servants; some are beaten and some are killed. Then the owner sends his son, his "beloved son," because he believes they will respect him. But instead, when the son, the heir, arrives, the tenants, thinking to have the vineyard for themselves, kill him also.

Commonly called the parable of the wicked tenants, this story ~not Jesus? might better be called the parable of the *greedy* tenants. Of course, they are wicked: they kill people. But the motivation for their murderous behavior is greed: they want to possess the produce of the vineyard for themselves.

As many of the parables of Jesus do, the story concludes with an invitation to its hearers to make a judgment about what they have just heard. Jesus asks, "What then will the owner of the vineyard do?" Jesus supplies the obvious answer: "He will come and destroy the tenants and give the vineyard to others."

Christian interpretation of this parable has most often emphasized a christological meaning, as if its purpose is to proclaim that Jesus is the "beloved son" sent by the vineyard owner, who symbolizes God. Much scholarly endeavor has been expended on this issue. Some scholars argue that the parable goes back to Jesus and is thus evidence that the historical Jesus saw himself as the beloved Son of God. Other scholars argue that Jesus did not make such a claim for himself and thus suspect that the parable is a post-Easter creation by the early Christian movement.

We do not need to enter into this debate, for our focus is on what the parable means as part of Mark's story of Jesus's final week. Although for the author of Mark Jesus is of course the Son of God, the primary meaning of the parable is not christological. Rather, as Mark tells us at the very end of the story, it is an indictment of the authorities: "They realized that he had told this parable against them." "They" refers to the chief priests, elders, and scribes of the previous episode, those at the top of the local domination system. They are the greedy and murderous tenants who rejected and killed the servants and son sent by the owner of the vineyard.

Because of the long Christian tradition that "the Jews" rejected Jesus, Christians have often surmised that the wicked and greedy tenants are the Jewish people as a whole. We emphasize, however, that the identification of the tenants with the Jewish people is both profoundly and wickedly wrong. The *tenants* are not "Israel," not "the Jews." Rather, the *vineyard* is Israel—both the land and its people. And the vineyard belongs to God, not to the greedy tenants—the powerful and wealthy at the top of the local domination system—who want its produce for themselves.

Realizing that Jesus told this parable against them, the authorities want to arrest him. But they do not, despite their desire to do so. The reason: "They feared the crowd." The crowd is on the side of Jesus.

TAXES TO CAESAR?

Then they sent to him some Pharisees and some Herodians to trap him in what he said. And they came and said to him, "Teacher, we know that you are sincere, and show deference to no one; for you do not regard people with partiality, but teach the way of God in accordance with truth. Is it lawful to pay taxes to the emperor, or not? Should we pay them, or should we not?" But knowing their hypocrisy, he said to them, "Why are you putting me to the test? Bring me a denarius and let me see it." And they brought one. Then he said to them, "Whose head is this, and whose title?" They answered, "The emperor's." Jesus said to them, "Give to the emperor the things that are the emperor's, and to God the things that are God's." And they were utterly amazed at him.

MARK 12:13–17

—— ◆ ——

The next confrontation, in 12:13–17, climaxes with perhaps the best-known verse from Mark's story of Tuesday. In the language of an earlier translation, "Render to Caesar the things that are Caesar's, and to God the things that are God's."

As often happens in the interpretation of the Bible, there is a habituated way of seeing this passage that gets in the way of seeing its meaning in the context of Mark's story of Jesus's last week. In the centuries after the gospels became "sacred scripture" for Christians, they (and the New Testament as a whole) were often read as "divine pronouncements" about doctrinal and ethical issues central to the Christian life.

Once this had happened, "Render to Caesar the things that are Caesar's, and to God the things that are God's" was understood as a solemn statement about the relationship between civil and religious authority, between politics and religion, or, in Christian terms, between "church and state." It has been most commonly understood to mean that there are two separate realms of human life, one religious and one political. In the first, we are to "render to God," and in the second, we are to "render to Caesar."

What this means in practice has varied considerably. It has been understood to mean absolute obedience to the state, notoriously by the majority of German Christians during the Hitler years. But the attitude is far more common. Long before the modern era, monarchs and their supporters used this verse to legitimate their authority: their subjects were to obey them because Jesus said that their political obligation belonged to the ruler's realm. More recently, many American Christians used it during the civil rights era to criticize acts of civil disobedience. This verse, they argued, means that we are to be obedient to civil authority, even if we might also want to modify its laws.

Some use it today to argue that Christians in the United States must support the government's decision to go to war with Iraq: in political matters, we are to obey our government. Other Christians do not argue for absolute obedience to government, regardless of its character, but nevertheless think that the verse does mean that religious obligation and political obligation are (and should be) basically separate.

But the heavy weight given to this verse as a solemn pronouncement about the relationship between religion and politics obscures what it means in Mark. The story in which the verse appears continues the series of verbal confrontations between Jesus and his opponents. The stories are marked by attack, parry, and counterattack, by trap, escape, and countertrap. To imagine that their purpose is to provide a set of eternal truths about how human life should be ordered is to ignore the larger narrative of which they are a part.

Seeking to set aside this habituated way of seeing this story, we return to the narrative. People identified as "some Pharisees" and "some Herodians" are sent to Jesus by the authorities. The Pharisees were a Jewish movement committed to an intensification of traditional religious practices, including sabbath observance and purity laws. Not only were these part of the covenant with God given to Moses at Mt. Sinai, but they were a form of resistance to assimilation to Hellenistic and Roman cultural imperialism. Though we know very little about the Herodians, they were, as the name implies, supporters of the Herods, the royal family of client-rulers appointed by Rome. Both here and earlier in his gospel (3:6; 8:15), Mark reports that these two groups were allied with each other and in league with the authorities.

They ask Jesus a question intended to trap him in what he said. They begin with a fawning prologue: "Teacher, we know that you are sincere, and show deference to no one. For you do not regard people with partiality, but teach the way of God in accordance with truth." Then they ask him, "Is it lawful to pay taxes to the emperor or not?" Is it lawful to pay taxes to Caesar? "Should we pay them, or should we not?"

It was a volatile question. Ever since the Jewish homeland had been added to the Roman Empire in 63 BCE, Rome had required a large annual "tribute" from the Jewish people. Rome did not collect tribute directly from its individual subjects. Rather, local authorities were responsible for its payment and collection (and in our passage, it is they who send the Pharisees and Herodians to Jesus).

Though tribute included the per capita, or "head," tax levied on all adult Jewish men, the annual sum due to Rome included much more. Most of this was gathered through taxes on land and agricultural production. All of this together contributed to "tribute" to Rome. It was the way the empire profited from its possessions.

Roman taxation was onerous not only because it was economically burdensome. It also symbolized the Jewish homeland's lack of sovereignty. It underlined the oppression of the Jews by an alien lord, as the word "tribute" itself suggests.

The spokesmen of the authorities set the trap skillfully. Either answer would get Jesus in trouble. If Jesus were to answer no, he could be charged with advocating denial of Roman authority—in short, with sedition. If he were to answer yes, he risked discrediting himself with the crowd, who for both economic and religious reasons resented Roman rule and taxation. Most likely, this was the primary purpose of the question: to separate Jesus from the crowd by leading him into an unpopular response.

Jesus's response is masterful. As he did in the question about authority, he turns the situation back on his opponents. He sets a countertrap when he asks to see a denarius. A denarius was a silver coin equal to approximately a day's wage. His interrogators produce one. Jesus looks at it and then asks, "Whose head is this, and whose title?" Or in the words of an older translation, "Whose image and inscription is this?" We all know their answer: "The emperor's."

Jesus's strategy has led his questioners to disclose to the crowd that they have a coin with Caesar's image on it. In this moment, they are discredited. Why? In the Jewish homeland in the first century, there were two types of coins. One type, because of the Jewish prohibition of graven images, had no human or animal images. The second type (including Roman coinage) had images. Many Jews would not carry or use coins of the second type. But Jesus's interrogators in the story did. The coin they produced had Caesar's image along with the standard and idolatrous inscription heralding Caesar as divine and Son of God. They are exposed as part of the politics of collaboration. Jesus's rhetorical strategy is brilliant: their trap has been evaded, his own countertrap set and sprung.

Thus, even before the famous words about rendering to Caesar, Jesus has won the encounter. But there is more: he responds to their initial question. His response is in two parallel halves:

1. Give to the emperor the things that are the emperor's.

2. Give to God the things that are God's.

Following immediately upon the disclosure that they are carrying a coin with Caesar's image, the first half of the saying means simply, "It's Caesar's coin—give it back to him."

This is in effect a nonanswer to the larger question, "Should we pay taxes to Caesar?" It cannot be seen as an endorsement of paying taxes to Rome or of Rome's rule. If Jesus had wanted to say, "Pay taxes to Caesar," he could simply have answered yes to their question. There would have been no need for the scene with the coin, the central element of the story.

The nonanswer is not simply a dismissal of the issue, however. The second half of Jesus's response is both evocative and provocative: "Give to God the things that are God's." It raises the question, "What belongs to Caesar, and what belongs to God?" For Jesus and many of his Jewish contemporaries, everything belongs to God. So their sacred scripture affirmed. The land of Israel belongs to God—recall Leviticus 25:23, which says

that all are tenant farmers or resident aliens on land that belongs to God. To use Tuesday's language, the vineyard belongs
to God, not to the local collaborators, not to Rome. Indeed, the
whole earth belongs to God: "The earth is the Lord's and the
fullness thereof" (Ps. 24:1). What belongs to Caesar? The im-
plication is, nothing.

GOD OF THE DEAD OR OF THE LIVING?

Some Sadducees, who say there is no resurrection, came to
him and asked him a question, saying, "Teacher, Moses
wrote for us that if a man's brother dies, leaving a wife but
no child, the man shall marry the widow and raise up children for his brother. There were seven brothers; the first
married and, when he died, left no children; and the second
married her and died, leaving no children; and the third
likewise; none of the seven left children. Last of all the
woman herself died. In the resurrection whose wife will she
be? For the seven had married her."

Jesus said to them, "Is not this the reason you are wrong,
that you know neither the scriptures nor the power of God?
For when they rise from the dead, they neither marry nor
are given in marriage, but are like angels in heaven. And as
for the dead being raised, have you not read in the book of
Moses, in the story about the bush, how God said to him, 'I
am the God of Abraham, the God of Isaac, and the God of
Jacob'? He is God not of the dead, but of the living; you are
quite wrong."

MARK 12:18–27

———— • ◆ • ————

Mark tells us in 12:18–27 that some Sadducees come to Jesus.
The Sadducees were part of the aristocracy. Wealthy and powerful,
they included high-priestly families as well as lay nobility. As a

group, they overlap but are not identical to the "chief priests, elders, and scribes" who have been central to Tuesday's stories thus far.

Their religious convictions differed in two significant ways from those of most of their Jewish contemporaries. First, they accepted only the "law" ("the five books of Moses," also called the Torah or Pentateuch) as sacred scripture, whereas most Jews also saw "the prophets" as sacred. Their nonacceptance of the prophets reflected their position in society, for the books of the prophets emphasize God's justice over against the human injustice of social systems dominated by the wealthy and powerful.

Second, as Mark's story tells us, the Sadducees did not believe in an afterlife. That is, in Jewish terms, they did not believe there would be a resurrection of the dead. Within Judaism, the belief in a life after death was a relatively recent development. It emerged some two centuries earlier with the martyrdom of faithful Jews who resisted the Hellenistic emperor Antiochus Epiphanes IV. Its purpose was to redress human injustice: Jews who were faithful to God were being executed, and Jews who were willing to collaborate with Antiochus were being spared. Thus belief in a resurrection was a way of defending God's justice: the martyrs would receive a blessed afterlife. By the time of Jesus, a majority of Jews (including deeply committed groups like the Pharisees and Essenes) affirmed a life after death. So apparently did Jesus, even though life after death was not the focus of his message.

But the Sadducees did not. Their privileged place in society meant that they had little or no awareness of any serious injustice that needed to be rectified. As one of our graduate school professors put it, "If you're rich and powerful, who needs an afterlife?"

The afterlife is the subject of the question they bring to Jesus. Given that they didn't believe in one, their purpose is obviously not a desire for information about what it will be like. Rather, as with the previous interrogators, their purpose is to discredit Jesus in the presence of the crowd. So they pose a conundrum to which they imagine no intelligent response is possible.

They begin by referring to a Jewish practice known as levirate marriage, in which, if a man dies before his wife has a child, then the man's brother shall marry the widow and conceive an heir for the brother who died. A child conceived under these conditions is understood to be the offspring of the dead brother. The practice flowed out of the primary purposes of patriarchal marriage: progeny and property. The concern is the transmission of the man's genetic material, name, and property, and the wife is handed on from brother to brother to serve this purpose.

Then they tell a story about seven brothers each of whom marries a woman in succession. They want to know whose wife she will be in the afterlife. For those who think of life after death as more or less a continuation or restoration of this life, including the relationships we have in this life, it was (and continues to be) a reasonable question. Does personal identity continue in a life after death, and do our relationships continue? Are families reunited? If so, whose wife will she be?

Jesus's response is threefold. His first response is a broad indictment of the Sadducees. He charges them with a deficient understanding of scripture and God: "You know neither the scriptures nor the power of God" (12:24).

His second response addresses the specific question they have asked about whose wife she will be. Jesus says, "When they rise from the dead, they neither marry nor are given in marriage, but are like angels in heaven" (12:25).

It is unclear to us what to make of this response. Is it intended (by Jesus or Mark) as an informative statement about the afterlife—namely, that there will be no marriage there, for we will be "like angels"? If so, what does this mean? What does it mean to be "like angels," and how does this connect to absence of marriage? Is the life of the age to come sexless, perhaps even genderless? Or does being "like angels" mean that procreation and property—the primary purposes of patriarchal and levirate marriage—are irrelevant there? Or does it mean even more—namely, that conditions in the resurrected life will be radically different from what life is like on earth? And how radical is the discontinuity? Will we still be "us"?

Or is the attempt to discern an informative meaning basically a mistake? Is Jesus's response, as in some of the previous stories, intended primarily as a skillful evasion of a question intended to entrap him? Is it perhaps intended not to inform, but to confound?

In his third response, Jesus refers to a passage from the book of Exodus, one of the books the Sadducees did regard as sacred scripture. He quotes the voice of God in the story about Moses's experience of God in the burning bush: "I am the God of Abraham, the God of Isaac, and the God of Jacob" (Exod. 3:6). Then Jesus adds, "God is God not of the dead, but of the living. You are quite wrong" (12:27).

As with Jesus's second response, we are puzzled about what to make of this. Is it meant to be a substantial claim about the afterlife—not only that there is one, but that Abraham, Isaac, and Jacob are still alive? Or, within this series of challenge and riposte stories, are we to hear this statement as another example of brilliant repartee, a provocative "nonresponse"?

Against the first possibility, we note that the story of Moses at the bush was never used within Judaism as an argument for an afterlife, and we cannot imagine that Jesus thought his opponents would be impressed with it. Moreover, if we hear Jesus's words about Abraham, Isaac, and Jacob as a substantial claim about an afterlife, it would mean that Jesus thought they were already in an afterlife, despite the fact that Jewish belief in the resurrection of the dead saw it as a future happening in time, quite different from Greek notions of immortality in a beyond that is above time.

So we are inclined to see his response as yet another example of Jesus's fending off his opponents' attacks with a debating skill that confounded them even as it delighted the crowd. And perhaps there is a bit more as well. Jesus's concluding words, "God is God not of the dead, but of the living," are tantalizingly evocative. His words suggest that God's concern is the living and not the dead. To think that Jesus's message and passion were about what happens to the dead, and to ask questions about the fate of the dead, is to miss the point. For Jesus, the kingdom of God is not primarily about the dead, but about the living, not primarily about life after death, but about life in this world.

THE GREAT COMMANDMENT

One of the scribes came near and heard them disputing with one another, and seeing that he answered them well, he asked him, "Which commandment is the first of all?" Jesus answered, "The first is, 'Hear, O Israel: the Lord our God, the Lord is one; you shall love the Lord your God with all your heart, and with all your soul, and with all your mind, and with all your strength.' The second is this, 'You shall love your neighbor as yourself.' There is no other commandment greater than these." Then the scribe said to him, "You are right, Teacher; you have truly said that 'he is one, and besides him there is no other'; and 'to love him with all the heart, and with all the understanding, and with all the strength,' and 'to love one's neighbor as oneself,'—this is much more important than all whole burnt offerings and sacrifices." When Jesus saw that he answered wisely, he said to him, "You are not far from the kingdom of God." After that no one dared to ask him any question.

MARK 12:28–34

For the first and only time in this section of Mark, the theme of conflict disappears, and we have a story in 12:28–34 in which a connection is made between Jesus and an interrogator. A scribe, "seeing that Jesus answered them well," asks, "Which command-ment is the first of all?" As Matthew narrates the same encounter, he attributes the question to a Pharisee with a hostile motive who wishes to "test" Jesus (Matt. 22:34–35). But not so in Mark, where the questioner is impressed with Jesus.

"Which commandment is the first of all?" It's an important question. What is most central? What matters most? What is the character of God? What does it mean to take God seriously?

A request to provide a concise summary of what loyalty to God means was not unusual within Judaism, though teachers were not always ready to be brief. According to a story reported in the Talmud, a Gentile asked two of the best-known Pharisaic teachers in the first century, Shammai and Hillel, to teach him the whole of the Torah while standing on one foot. Shammai drove him away with a stick, because, he said, the Torah cannot be crystallized. But Hillel responded, "What is hateful to you, do not do to your neighbor. That is the whole Torah, while the rest is commentary thereon; go and learn it" (*b. Sabbat* 31a).

Like Hillel and unlike Shammai, Jesus does not refuse the re-quest. He quotes two passages from the Jewish Bible, both from the Torah. From Deuteronomy, he cites the classic Jewish affirmation of loyalty to God: "Hear, O Israel: the Lord our God, the Lord is one; you shall love the Lord your God with all your heart, and with all your soul, and with all your mind, and with all your strength" (6:5–6). Jews recited this text twice daily during morning and evening prayers. It was also put into small containers that were mounted on doorposts (*mezuzot*) and worn on the arm and head (*tefillin*, or "phylacteries"). Then Jesus quotes a second passage, this one from Leviticus: "You shall love your neighbor as yourself" (19:18).

The twofold great commandment—to love God and love our neighbor—is so familiar to us that it has become a Christian cliché. But behind the familiarity is their radical meaning as Jesus's summary of his message. To love God above all else means giving to God what belongs to God: our heart, soul, mind, and strength. These belong to God, and (to refer to a previous episode) not to Caesar. This is radical monotheism: if God is Lord, then the lords of this world—Caesar and his incarnations throughout history—are not. And to love one's neighbor as one's self means to refuse to accept the divisions rendered by the normalcy of civilization, those divisions between the respected and the marginalized, righteous and sinners, rich and poor, friends and enemies, Jews and Gentiles.

Jesus's radical combination of these two commands from Jewish scripture elicits a positive response from the scribe: "You are right, Teacher." Then the scribe repeats what he has just heard from Jesus, with a striking addition: "This is much more important than all whole burnt offerings and sacrifices." Thus the scribe brings up the contrast that dominates this section of Mark: Jesus's conflict with the temple authorities and their representatives. In the court of the temple, the scribe affirms that following these two commandments matters much more than the temple and what happens there.

In the midst of this series of conflict stories, we are reminded that not all scribes were opposed to Jesus, just as not all Pharisees and aristocrats were. Later in Mark's gospel Joseph of Arimathea, a wealthy member of the council, arranges for the burial of Jesus. Moreover, Luke reports some friendly Pharisees as well as women supporters who were wives of high-ranking members of Herod's court (13:31; 8:1–3).

To return to the scribe of Mark's story, Jesus affirms his affirmation: "Jesus saw that he had answered wisely." Then, in words that assert both nearness and distance, Jesus says to him: "You are not far from the kingdom of God" (12:34). He is not far from it because he knows its heart, but he is not in it. To be in it means more than knowing this. It means living it.

JESUS CHALLENGES
SCRIBAL TEACHING AND PRACTICE

While Jesus was teaching in the temple, he said, "How can the scribes say that the Messiah is the son of David? David himself, by the Holy Spirit, declared, 'The Lord said to my Lord, "Sit at my right hand, until I put your enemies under your feet."' David himself calls him Lord; so how can he be his son?" And the large crowd was listening to him with delight.

As he taught, he said, "Beware of the scribes, who like to walk around in long robes, and to be greeted with respect in the marketplaces, and to have the best seats in the synagogues and places of honor at banquets! They devour widows' houses and for the sake of appearance say long prayers. They will receive the greater condemnation."

He sat down opposite the treasury, and watched the crowd putting money into the treasury. Many rich people put in large sums. A poor widow came and put in two small copper coins, which are worth a penny. Then he called his disciples and said to them, "Truly I tell you, this poor widow has put in more than all those who are contributing to the treasury. For all of them have contributed out of their abundance; but she out of her poverty has put in everything she had, all she had to live on."

MARK 12:35–44

———— ✦ ————

The theme of conflict resumes in 12:35–44, even as the format changes. Thus far Jesus's interrogators have set the topics; they have questioned Jesus about his authority, taxes to Caesar, resurrection, and the greatest commandment. Now Jesus takes the initiative.

Still in the temple, he challenges scribal teaching. He asks, "How can the scribes say that the Messiah is the son of David?" Then, citing the Jewish tradition that King David wrote the

Psalms, he quotes Psalm 110:1: "David himself, by the Holy Spirit, declared, 'The Lord said to my Lord, "Sit at my right hand, until I put your enemies under your feet."' David himself calls him Lord; so how can he be his son?"

In its original setting in the book of Psalms, the first use of the word "Lord" refers to God, and the second use to the king of Israel. God says to the king, "Sit at my right hand until I make your enemies your footstool." During the time of the monarchy, the psalm was used in the coronation or enthronement of a king. It promised God's aid to the king in defeating his enemies.

By the first century, however, this psalm was understood as a messianic psalm, so that the second use of the word "Lord" was now understood to refer to the Messiah. Hence the concluding comment and question: "David himself calls him [the Messiah] Lord; so how can he be his son?" The question challenges the teaching of the scribes that the Messiah is the son of David. But what does this mean? What does "son of David" mean here?

One possibility is that it is about biological ancestry. If so, it seems to deny that the Messiah is descended from David and thus implies that Jesus (who is, of course, the Messiah, according to Mark) is not of Davidic descent. But this seems unlikely. Though Mark does not tell us about Jesus's ancestry, the tradition that Jesus was descended from David is early. Paul refers to it (Rom. 1:3), as do the stories of Jesus's birth and genealogies in Matthew and Luke, which are independent of each other.

Another possibility is that "son of David" is a messianic category here, not a biological one. Some of Jesus's contemporaries expected that the Messiah would be "son of David" in the sense of being a king like David—a warrior who presided over Israel in the time of its greatest power and glory. This seems more likely. The message here then is that the Messiah will not be a king like David, not "son of David" in this sense. Rather, the Messiah will be the kind of king symbolized by Jesus's entry into Jerusalem at the beginning of the final week.

Yet "son of David" is not completely a negative category in Mark. It is used in two previous stories without repudiation. In Jericho, as Jesus nears Jerusalem, the blind beggar Bartimaeus twice calls out to Jesus, "Son of David, have compassion on me" (10:47). In the story of Jesus's entry into Jerusalem, those who welcome Jesus shout, "Blessed is the coming kingdom of our ancestor David!" (11:10). In neither story does Mark indicate that this language is inappropriate. And even earlier in Mark, Jesus refers to an action of David's to justify the behavior of his disciples (2:23–26).

Thus it seems that term "son of David" is not so much wrong as inadequate. The point, rather, is that the Messiah is *David's Lord*—that is, greater than David, more than David, different from David. So also the kingdom of which Jesus speaks is greater than David's, more than David's, different from David's.

No scribal response is reported to Jesus's riddlelike question. But the crowd loves it: "And the large crowd was listening to him with delight."

Then Jesus indicts the self-important practice of the scribes— they like to wear long robes, expect recognition of their status in public places, and say long prayers for the sake of appearances. And yet, "They devour widows' houses" (12:40). Throughout the Hebrew Bible, widows (along with orphans) are special objects of God's compassion, for, without a man to provide for them, they were the most vulnerable people. Their treatment was a measure of the justice or injustice of the society.

How do the scribes devour widows' houses? Most likely, the reference is to the scribes' activity as a literate class working for the wealthy; they would have administered loan agreements and then foreclosed on widows' property when the loan could not be repaid.

The indictment of the scribes for their treatment of widows is followed immediately by a story about a poor widow who puts into the temple treasury "all she had" (two small copper coins). Jesus contrasts her gift with the gifts of the wealthy. Though they put in large sums of money, they do so "out of their abundance."

The poor widow, out of her poverty, puts in "everything she had, all she had to live on" (12:44).

Most commonly, this passage is understood as contrasting the deep devotion of the poor widow with the public display of generosity of the wealthy. As such, she (rather than the wealthy) is a positive image of discipleship: she gave all that she had. An alternative interpretation hears the passage as a condemnation of the way the poor are manipulated to give all that they have to support the temple. It does not condemn the widow, but the system that leads her to act this way. In either case, the passage is critical of the wealthy.

after the widows story - this is God's response

✗ THE TEMPLE'S DESTRUCTION AND JESUS'S RETURN

the look of justice

As he came out of the temple, one of his disciples said to him, "Look, Teacher, what large stones and what large buildings!" Then Jesus asked him, "Do you see these great buildings? Not one stone will be left here upon another; all will be thrown down."

When he was sitting on the Mount of Olives opposite the temple, Peter, James, John, and Andrew asked him privately, "Tell us, when will this be, and what will be the sign that all these things are about to be accomplished?"

MARK 13:1–4

———— • ◆ • ————

Jesus and his disciples now leave the temple in 13:1. Standing outside the temple platform, they can see the massive stones used in the construction of its walls. One of the disciples exclaims about their huge size: "Look, Teacher, what large stones and what large buildings!"

The exclamation is warranted. Josephus reports that the largest stones measured 68 feet long, 9 feet high, and 8 feet wide. Historians have noted that Josephus often inflates his numbers, but in this case archaeological excavation confirms that the stones used in the construction of the temple's walls were huge. The largest one found so far is 40 feet long, 10 feet high, and 14 feet wide, with an estimated weight of 500 tons. One might imagine that the temple was indeed indestructible.

But Jesus responds, in effect, "Are you impressed with these great buildings?" Then he says, "Not one stone will be left upon another; all will be thrown down" (13:2). Like the prophet Jeremiah some six centuries earlier, Jesus speaks of the destruction of the temple. The destruction will also include Jerusalem, of course. In an important sense, this passage is the climax of the series of conflicts between Jesus and the system of domination and collaboration centered in the temple. The judgment against what it had become pronounced by Jesus's prophetic act in the temple on Monday is here explicitly articulated. And, it is important to remind ourselves, the judgment against the temple is not a judgment against Judaism or against ritual, but against the temple as "a den of robbers."

The next two verses, 13:3–4, are a transition to the rest of the chapter (13:5–37). The setting shifts from the temple to the Mount of Olives. Presumably Jesus and his disciples are on their way to Bethany, just east of Jerusalem, where they will spend the night (14:3). Yet the temple is still very much in view. From the Mount of Olives, there is a panoramic view of Jerusalem with the temple mount in the foreground. There some of Jesus's disciples ask him, "When will this be, and what will be the sign that all these things are about to be accomplished?" The use of the singular in the first half of the question—"When will *this* be"—refers back to the destruction of the temple, and the use of the plural in the second half—"*all these things*"—refers forward to the rest of the chapter.

THE LITTLE APOCALYPSE

Then Jesus began to say to them, "Beware that no one leads you astray. Many will come in my name and say, 'I am he!'

and they will lead many astray. When you hear of wars and rumors of wars, do not be alarmed; this must take place, but the end is still to come. For nation will rise against nation, and kingdom against kingdom; there will be earthquakes in various places; there will be famines. This is but the beginning of the birth pangs.

"As for yourselves, beware; for they will hand you over to councils; and you will be beaten in synagogues; and you will stand before governors and kings because of me, as a testimony to them. And the good news must first be proclaimed to all nations. When they bring you to trial and hand you over, do not worry beforehand about what you are to say; but say whatever is given you at that time, for it is not you who speak, but the Holy Spirit. Brother will betray brother to death, and a father his child, and children will rise against parents and have them put to death; and you will be hated by all because of my name. But the one who endures to the end will be saved.

"But when you see the desolating sacrilege set up where it ought not to be (let the reader understand), then those in Judea must flee to the mountains; the one on the housetop must not go down or enter the house to take anything away; the one in the field must not turn back to get a coat. Woe to those who are pregnant and to those who are nursing infants in those days! Pray that it may not be in winter. For in those days there will be suffering, such as has not been from the beginning of the creation that God created until now, no, and never will be. And if the Lord had not cut short those days, no one would be saved; but for the sake of the elect, whom he chose, he has cut short those days. And if anyone says to you at that time, 'Look! Here is the Messiah!' or 'Look! There he is!'—do not believe it. False messiahs and false prophets will appear and produce signs and omens, to lead astray, if possible, the elect. But be alert; I have already told you everything.

"But in those days, after that suffering, the sun will be darkened, and the moon will not give its light, and the stars will be falling from heaven, and the powers in the heavens will be shaken. Then they will see 'the Son of Man coming in clouds' with great power and glory. Then he will send out the angels, and gather his elect from the four winds, from the ends of the earth to the ends of heaven.

"From the fig tree learn its lesson: as soon as its branch becomes tender and puts forth its leaves, you know that summer is near. So also, when you see these things taking place, you know that he is near, at the very gates. Truly I tell you, this generation will not pass away until all these things have taken place. Heaven and earth will pass away, but my words will not pass away.

"But about that day or hour no one knows, neither the angels in heaven, nor the Son, but only the Father. Beware, keep alert; for you do not know when the time will come. It is like a man going on a journey, when he leaves home and puts his slaves in charge, each with his work, and commands the doorkeeper to be on the watch. Therefore, keep awake—for you do not know when the master of the house will come, in the evening, or at midnight, or at cockcrow, or at dawn, or else he may find you asleep when he comes suddenly. And what I say to you I say to all: Keep awake."

MARK 13:5–37

———— ◆ ————

Mark 13:5–37 is commonly called the "little apocalypse." The "big apocalypse" is, of course, the book of Revelation. An apocalypse—the word means "revelation" or "unveiling"—is a kind of Jewish and Christian literature that reveals or unveils the future in language loaded with images and symbols. Apocalyptic literature speaks of a time of great suffering followed by divine deliverance. The little apocalypse takes the form of a long discourse by

Jesus, indeed the longest single speech in Mark's gospel. Its fore-
told events include:

- False messiahs and false prophets

- Wars and rumors of wars

- Earthquakes and famines

- Persecution by authorities: councils, synagogues, governors,
  and kings

- A "desolating sacrilege" where it should not be

- A time of suffering greater than there's ever been

- Cosmic disorder: darkened sun, no light from the moon,
  stars falling from the sky

- The Son of Man coming on clouds with great power and
  glory, and his angels gathering the elect from the four ends
  of the earth

Specific warnings include:

- Beware that no one leads you astray.

- Flee to the mountains.

- Keep alert—watch—keep awake.

At the center of the little apocalypse is an event described as
"the desolating sacrilege set up where it ought not to be," followed by an aside to the reader, the only such remark in Mark:
"Let the reader understand" (13:14). The description makes use of
language from an earlier Jewish apocalypse, the second half of the
book of Daniel, where it refers to the seizure and desecration of
the temple by the gentile emperor Antiochus Epiphanes two centuries earlier.

Chapter 13 uses this language to speak of an event in Mark's own time, namely, the conquest and destruction of Jerusalem and the temple by Rome in the year 70. At the climax of their conquest, Roman troops offered a sacrifice to the Roman emperor in the temple. From this, it follows that the warnings in the chapter—of wars and rumors of wars, nation rising against nation and kingdom against kingdom, false messiahs and false prophets, persecution and suffering—are associated with the war that led to the destruction of Jerusalem and the temple.

The war began in the year 66 when the greatest of the Jewish revolts against Roman rule broke out. The Jewish freedom fighters were successful for a while. Jerusalem, the center of local collaboration, had now become the center of violent resistance to Rome. It took Rome four years to reconquer Jerusalem, and another three or four years to eliminate the last of Jewish resistance at Masada. The whole period was a time of great suffering for Jews, including Jewish Christians. In areas of the Jewish homeland and nearby countries with significant Jewish populations, Gentiles persecuted and sometimes massacred Jews. Factional strife among Jewish rebel groups added to the carnage. Great numbers of Jews were killed by the Romans as they reconquered the Jewish homeland, perhaps as high a percentage of the Jewish people as perished under Hitler.

These correlations between Mark 13 and the great war are the primary reason for dating Mark around the year 70, whether shortly before the destruction of the temple or shortly afterward. The flames of the great war cast shadows on Mark even as they illuminate Mark.

Mark addresses his community in these circumstances. Of course, Mark is addressing his community throughout his gospel, but especially in chapter 13. Though his community was geographically some distance from Jerusalem, most likely in the north of Galilee, it was very much affected by the war. The northern part of the Jewish homeland was reconquered by the Romans early in the war. Yet persecution and massacres of Jews by Gentiles in local areas continued.

Moreover, the central commitment of Mark's community intensified its difficulty. As followers of Jesus, they were an anti-imperial movement and yet committed to nonviolence. Jesus's central message was the "kingdom of God," which placed them in opposition to the imperial domination system. And yet, following Jesus, they were also committed to nonviolence, which set them apart from the resistance movement. Jews (including Jewish Christians) were under pressure to join the war against Rome. People thought to be collaborators were killed by the rebels and people thought to be rebels were killed by the Romans. To be neither made one suspect in both camps. And thus Mark 13 warns Jesus's followers of persecution.

The warning of "the desolating sacrilege set up where it ought not to be" is followed by a series of imperatives:

Those in Judea must flee to the mountains.

The one on the housetop must not go down or enter the house to take anything away.

The one in the field must not turn back to get a coat.

In this setting, these are counsels to get away from the invasion and to make haste—flee quickly! The point is *not* to become part of the violence, *not* to join in the battle for Jerusalem. The imperatives are consistent with the nonviolence of Jesus and early Christianity. Importantly, it was not nonviolence as a passive withdrawal from the world, not nonviolence as nonresistance to evil, but nonviolence as a way of resisting evil. These early Christians were both anti-imperial and nonviolent.

But the desolating sacrilege—the devastation of the temple—is not the last word in this chapter. For Jesus also speaks of the "coming of the Son of Man." The passage begins with a time indicator: "But in those days, *after* that suffering," that is, *after* the great war:

> "The sun will be darkened, and the moon will not give its light, and the stars will be falling from heaven, and the powers of the heavens will be shaken. Then they will see 'the Son of Man coming in clouds' with great power and glory. Then he will send out the angels, and gather his elect from the four winds, from the ends of the earth to the ends of heaven." (13:24–27)

Once again, language from the apocalyptic portion of Daniel is used: "the Son of Man coming in clouds" echoes Daniel 7:13. There it refers to a humanlike figure who comes *to* God and to whom God gives an everlasting kingdom. But in Mark 13, "Son of Man" refers to an individual ("he") who comes "in clouds" *from* God. Almost certainly, Mark means that Jesus is "the Son of Man" who will come "'in clouds' with great power and glory." To use later Christian language, this seems to be a "second coming" of Jesus text.

Mark expected this soon. After the passage about the coming of the Son of Man, Mark reports that Jesus said: "When you see *these things taking place,* you know that he [presumably the Son of Man] is near, at the very gates. Truly I tell you, this generation will not pass away until *all these things have taken place*" (13:29–30).

Like some other early Christians, including Paul and the authors of Matthew and Revelation, Mark expected the second coming of Jesus to be soon. "All these things," echoing the question of the disciples just before the little apocalypse (13:4), will happen before "this generation" has passed away.

Mark's gospel thus has an apocalyptic eschatology, a technical phrase that refers to the expectation of dramatic and decisive divine intervention in the near future, one so public that even non-believers will have to agree that it has happened. Whether this kind of eschatology goes back to Jesus himself is a separate question. We do not think that it does. We see it as most likely a post-Easter creation of the early Christian movement. In our judgment, Mark's gospel expresses an intensification of apocalyptic expectation triggered by the great war. But once again, our focus in this book is how Mark tells the story of Jesus and not the historical reconstruction of Jesus.

From the vantage point of history, Mark's expectation of the imminent coming of the Son of Man—the return of Jesus—was wrong. To say the obvious, it didn't happen. But beneath Mark's timetable, one may perceive a deeper meaning in his apocalyptic conviction. Namely, what has begun in Jesus will triumph, despite the tumult and resistance of this world.

From this vantage point—one of confidence and enduring hope—who can say that Mark's conviction is wrong? The struggle goes on. Many of us do not have the same confidence in divine intervention. But we can share the same passion and hope.

Tuesday has been a long day. By now, it is evening on the Mount of Olives. Darkness is coming on, a darkness that will deepen as the week continues to unfold. And as darkness falls, Mark commends us, "Be alert! Stay awake! Watch!"

———— ·•· ————

FOUR

WEDNESDAY

It was two days before the Passover and the festival of Unleavened Bread. The chief priests and the scribes were looking for a way to arrest Jesus by stealth and kill him; for they said, "Not during the festival, or there may be a riot among the people."

While he was at Bethany in the house of Simon the leper, as he sat at the table, a woman came with an alabaster jar of very costly ointment of nard, and she broke open the jar and poured the ointment on his head. But some were there who said to one another in anger, "Why was the ointment wasted in this way? For this ointment could have been sold for more than three hundred denarii, and the money given to the poor." And they scolded her. But Jesus said, "Let her alone; why do you trouble her? She has performed a good service for me. For you always have the poor with you, and you can show kindness to them whenever you wish; but you will not always have me. She has done what she could; she has anointed my body beforehand for its burial. Truly I tell you, wherever the good news is proclaimed in the whole world, what she has done will be told in remembrance of her."

Then Judas Iscariot, who was one of the twelve, went to the chief priests in order to betray him to them. When they heard it, they were greatly pleased, and promised to give

him money. So he began to look for an opportunity to betray him.

MARK 14:1–11

——— ·•· ———

Recall what we said at the start of Chapter 2 about Mark's use
of frames as a literary device for placing two subjects in dramatic interaction with one another so that readers should use
them to interpret each other. There, on Monday, the two subjects
were the symbolic destruction of the fig tree for not producing
fruit and the symbolic destruction of the temple for not producing justice. In other words, the events were in parallel and sym-
metry. Here, on Wednesday, there is another Markan frame, but
now the two subjects are in opposition and contrast. The structure is like this:

Incident A¹:	The need	Mark	= Matthew	= Luke
	for a traitor	14:1–2	26:3–5	22:1–2
Incident B:	The unnamed	Mark	= Matthew	
	woman	14:3–9	26:6–13	
Incident A²:	The advent	Mark	= Matthew	= Luke
	of a traitor	14:10–11	26:14–16	22:3–6

That literary contrast between the framed unit and the framing
ones is between believer and traitor, but the depth of that Markan
juxtaposition requires an understanding of what each person
achieved within the sequence of Mark's story about Jesus. It is,
after all, easy to see why *betraying* Jesus represents the worst action possible, but why does *anointing* Jesus imply the best?

One footnote. As so often happens when Matthew and Luke
are faced with a Markan intercalation, they simply erase it by
running the two frames together without any centrally framed
unit between them. For example, Matthew unifies the cursing
and withering of the fig tree as a single incident on Monday

(21:18–20) rather than following Mark, who divided it over Monday and Tuesday to frame the temple incident. Matthew insists that Jesus's command was immediately obeyed, "And the fig tree withered at once," and "when the disciples saw it, they were amazed, saying, 'How did the fig tree wither at once?'" In this present case, as you can see from the table above, Matthew follows Mark's framing technique but Luke runs the frames together and omits the framed section. Those changes confirm at least indirectly the deliberate nature of this Markan literary and theological device.

THE NEED FOR A TRAITOR

In a tradition that goes back centuries, Christians have most often portrayed the Jewish crowd around Jesus during his last days as rabidly and violently against him. We see it in Passion plays, the most famous of which is at Oberammergau in Bavaria. We also see it in the more recent liturgical practice in many churches in which the congregation plays the part of the crowd as the story of Jesus's trial is read. The congregation chants, "Crucify him, crucify him!" It is also central to Mel Gibson's film *The Passion of the Christ*.

What these portrayals fail to ask, however, is this. Why, if the Jewish crowd was so against Jesus, was it necessary to arrest him in the darkness of night with the help of a traitor from among Jesus's followers? Why not arrest him in broad daylight? And why do they need Judas? Indeed, the Markan Jesus himself prompts us to ask precisely those questions: "Jesus said to them, 'Have you come out with swords and clubs to arrest me as though I were a bandit? Day after day I was with you in the temple teaching, and you did not arrest me'" (14:48–49). So why arrest him now in this place and in this manner? This is a crucial question, and to answer it we look back at Mark's account from Sunday through Wednesday morning.

On *Sunday,* as you recall, Jesus's anti-imperial entry into Jerusalem evoked great enthusiasm.: "Many people spread their cloaks on the road, and others spread leafy branches they had cut in the fields. Then those who went ahead and those who followed were shouting, 'Hosanna! Blessed is the one who comes in the name of the Lord! Blessed is the coming kingdom of our ancestor David! Hosanna in the highest heaven!'" (11:8–10).

Those involved are not identified in any way beyond that vague term "many." We are not told and may begin to wonder how many is many? In any demonstration, how many is many?

On *Monday,* after Jesus cites the text of Jeremiah ("den of robbers") during the temple's symbolic destruction, Mark records this reaction: "When the chief priests and the scribes heard it, they kept looking for a way to kill him; for they were afraid of him, because the whole crowd was spellbound by his teaching" (11:18). We now have a clear disjunction between the high-priestly authorities who wish to execute Jesus and the "whole crowd" who are "spellbound by his teaching." But, of course, since Jesus has been proclaiming the *already present* kingdom of God against the *already present* kingdom of Rome, that spell-bound crowd is both the reason as well as the deterrent for high-priestly action against him.

It is neither accurate nor necessary to demonize the family of Annas, its current representative, Caiaphas, or the other high-priestly families to understand what is happening. The concern of those collaborative leaders is fairly stated in John 11:48: "If we let him go on like this, everyone will believe in him, and the Romans will come and destroy both our holy place and our nation." And, we might add, either crowds or Romans or both will destroy *them.*

Even apart from the content of any message from Jesus sub-versive of Roman law and order, however nonviolent it might have been, the very presence of enthusiastic crowds listening to whatever it was he said would have been deemed dangerous at any time, but especially at Passover. The only reason given by Josephus for Antipas's execution of John the Baptizer in his *Jewish Antiquities* is not the content of John's message, but the size of John's crowd: "When others too joined the crowds about him, because they were aroused to the highest degree by his sermons, Herod became alarmed. Eloquence that had so great an effect on mankind might lead to some form of sedition, for it looked as if they would be guided by John in everything that they did" (18.116–19).

In any case, to return to Mark's story, by Monday, the Jewish religious authorities want to have Jesus executed, but are deterred from action because "the whole crowd was spellbound by his teaching." That is after (and because of?) those two prophetic symbolic actions: first, his entrance into Jerusalem to establish God's nonviolence against imperial domination and, second, his entrance into the temple to establish God's justice against high-priestly collaboration.

On *Tuesday,* that preceding contrast between the Jewish authorities and the Jewish crowd is repeated three times—in case we might have missed it. First, after Jesus interrogated "the chief priests, the scribes, and the elders" concerning John the Baptizer, they were unable to answer negatively because "they were afraid of the crowd, for all regarded John as truly a prophet" (11:32). The crowd stands with both John and Jesus against their own religious authorities, who oppose them both. Next, Jesus tells the parable of the wicked tenants who murder the vineyard owner's son and, "when they realized that he had told this parable against them, they wanted to arrest him, but they feared the crowd. So they left him and went away" (12:12). Finally, Jesus challenges "the scribes" on how the Messiah can be both David's son and David's Lord at the same time, "and the large crowd was listening to him with delight" (12:37).

To see Mark's emphasis on Jesus as protected by the supporting crowd from action by the threatening authorities, it is necessary to understand the narrative logic of *Wednesday* morning. "It was two days before the Passover and the festival of Unleavened Bread. The chief priests and the scribes were looking for a way to arrest Jesus by stealth and kill him; for they said, 'Not during the festival, or there may be a riot among the people'" (14:1–2). In effect, the high-priestly authorities give up. They cannot arrest Jesus during the festival, and after it he will be gone. They give up—unless, of course, they can learn where he is apart from the crowd, arrest him apart from the crowd, and execute him before the crowd knows what is happening. Stealth is the last chance left. And that leaves 14:2 hanging for the arrival of Judas, the stealthy one, in 14:10.

Before we continue with Mark's account, how do the other evangelists portray the protective support of the crowd for Jesus from Sunday through Tuesday? Do the other evangelists follow Mark's emphasis? Less and less. Matthew has three of Mark's five in 21:8–9, 26, 46. Luke has three or possibly four of them in 19:37–38, 47 and 20:6, 19. The difficulty in Luke is in his account of Jesus's anti-imperial entry. He does not mention any "crowd" or "crowds," but speaks instead of "the whole multitude of the disciples." That is a rather ambiguous expression that *could* refer to the Jerusalem crowd as disciples, but *could* also be simply a way of referring to those who came from Galilee with Jesus. John, finally, has only one of Mark's five verses—the entry itself (12:12–18). In other words, as we move sequentially from Mark through Matthew and Luke to John, that is, from the early 70s to the mid 90s CE, that original emphasis on Jewish supporting crowd versus Jewish high-priestly authority diminishes significantly.

Finally, we note that the same distinction between the pro-Jesus Jewish crowd and the anti-Jesus Jewish authorities is cited in Josephus's comment about Jesus's life in his *Jewish Antiquities*. Jesus, he says, "won over many Jews and many of the Greeks. When Pilate, upon hearing him accused by men of the highest standing amongst us, had condemned him to be crucified, those who had in the first place come to love him did not give up their affection for him" (18.63–64).

THE TWELVE AS FAILED DISCIPLES

For us Lent is a transformative journey in time from Ash Wednesday to Easter Sunday. For Mark, "Lent" was a transformative journey in space from Caesarea Philippi to Jerusalem. During that journey, in Mark's story, Jesus tried to prepare his disciples for what would happen to him when he demonstrated against Roman imperial power concerning its violence and against Jewish high-priestly authority concerning its injustice. Also, and even more important, Jesus attempted to prepare them for their individual and communal participation in that death and resurrection, that end-as-beginning. But, as we shall see, Peter, James, and John, then the Twelve as a group, and finally Judas all fail tragically but not irrevocably (except for Judas) to accept their destiny alongside Jesus.

We emphasize and cannot emphasize enough one point about this very, very prominent theme in Mark. *His story of failed discipleship is his warning gift to all who ever hear or read his narrative.* We must think of Lent today as a penitential season because we know that, like those first disciples, we would like to avoid the implications of this journey with Jesus. We would like its Holy Week conclusion to be about the interior rather than the exterior life, about heaven rather than earth, about the future rather than the present, and, above all else, about religion safely and securely quarantined from politics. Confronting violent political power *and* unjust religious collaboration is dangerous in most times and most places, first century and twenty-first century alike. Here, then, is how Mark's warning builds up negatively toward the first person who positively believed Jesus's message—that unnamed woman with her eternal alabaster jar of ointment.

Very early in his story, Mark records that Jesus "went up the mountain and called to him those whom he wanted, and they came to him. And he appointed twelve, whom he also named apostles, to be with him, and to be sent out to proclaim the message. . . . So he appointed the twelve" (3:13–16). But there is a ferocious ambiguity in Mark's account of that group's relationship with Jesus. On the one hand, they are regularly taken aside for special instruction. In 9:28, for example, "when he had entered the house, his disciples asked him privately" about their inability to exorcize a demon, and in 10:10, "in the house the disciples asked him again about this matter" of no divorce. In 4:10, however, this separate group seems at least fleetingly larger than the twelve (disciples): "When he was alone, those who were around him along with the twelve asked him about the parables."

On the other hand, this special and separate instruction seems to be a dismal failure, seems, if anything, to increase their failure and even their responsibility for it. Thus Mark records of "the disciples" that "their hearts were hardened" (6:52), and Jesus upbraids them with this battery of accusatory questions: "Do you still not perceive or understand? Are your hearts hardened? Do you have eyes, and fail to see? Do you have ears, and fail to hear? And do you not remember?" (8:17–18). So, for general background, to be the Twelve (apostles or disciples) in Mark's story is to fail Jesus badly. And all of that becomes very, very specific on their "Lenten" journey with Jesus from Caesarea Philippi to Jerusalem. Indeed, in case we might miss what is already obvious enough internally, Mark frames that journey externally with the healing of a blind man at Bethsaida of Galilee before it began in 8:22–26 and again at Jericho of Judea in 10:46–52 as it ends. Between those frames of *blindness*, Mark focuses the failed discipleship of the Twelve around three prophetic warnings of his death and resurrection given to them by Jesus. In what follows watch always for this triple structure:

	First Warning	Second Warning	Third Warning
Prophecy by Jesus	8:31–32a	9:31	10:33–34
Reaction by the Twelve	8:32b	9:32–34	10:35–37
Response by Jesus	8:33–9:1	9:35–37	10:38–45

That threefold repetition by Mark emphasizes Jesus's insistence on what is to happen (*prophecy*), their failure to understand or accept it fully (*reaction*), and Jesus's explanation of what is involved for himself, for them, and for all his followers (*response*).

FIRST PROPHECY, REACTION, AND RESPONSE

Mark's Lenten journey starts at Caesarea Philippi, the capital city of Herod Philip's territories, in a venue as gentile as it was Jewish. Peter confesses that Jesus is the Messiah, but far from applauding him Jesus "sternly ordered them not to tell anyone about him" (8:29–30). Such injunctions to silence in Mark usually do *not* mean, "You have it right, but keep it secret," *but* rather, "You have it wrong, so keep it quiet." In other words, "Please, shut up!" Peter and the others may well have been imagining Jesus as a militant messiah who would free Israel from Roman oppression using violent means, and it was that notion that Jesus wanted to discourage.

But right after that wrong and silenced misunderstanding about Jesus as Messiah comes that correct and open announcement of Jesus as Son of Man: "Then he began to teach them that the Son of Man must undergo great suffering, and be rejected by the elders, the chief priests, and the scribes, and be killed, and after three days rise again. He said all this quite openly" (8:31–32a). Jesus names himself as *Son of Man*, and that title will be repeated in the second and third prophecies concerning his execution and resurrection that Jesus gives to the twelve disciples (9:31; 10:33–34), linking all three. That title comes to its climactic use in the trial scene in 14:62, and we discuss it more fully in Chapter 5.

All three connected prophecies of death and resurrection beget at least incomprehension if not downright opposition from the Twelve. The first one in 8:31–32a generates complete dismissal as "Peter took him aside and began to rebuke him" (8:32b). And Jesus's response is equally blunt: "But turning and looking at his disciples, he rebuked Peter and said, 'Get behind me, Satan! For you are setting your mind not on divine things but on human things'" (8:33).

Notice two details. That verb "rebuke," used first by Peter to Jesus and then by Jesus back to Peter, is a very, very strong one. It is, for example, the same verb used by Jesus against demons in 1:25 and 9:25. This is, in other words, a very serious matter. Any attempt to deter Jesus from his destiny is, in effect, demonic and Satanic. But the second item is equally important. That counter-rebuke by Jesus is not just addressed to Peter; Jesus turns and looks at his disciples, so that all of them are brought under that counterrebuke. It is not just for Peter, but for all the twelve disciples, and it is not just for them, but for everyone, as Mark deliberately widens the audience outward: "He called the crowd with his disciples" (8:34a). In other words, Mark proposes Jesus's Lenten journey as an open invitation for all. And here is what is at stake for everyone:

> "If any want to become my followers, let them deny themselves and take up their cross and follow me. For those who want to save their life will lose it, and those who lose their life for my sake, and for the sake of the gospel, will save it. For what will it profit them to gain the whole world and forfeit their life? Indeed, what can they give in return for their life?" (8:34b–37)

It is extremely important to underline Mark's theology at this point. For him, Jesus knows in precise detail what is going to happen, but he does not speak of suffering vicariously to atone for the sins of the world. Instead, Peter, the other members of the Twelve, and the "crowd" are all expected to walk with Jesus toward death and resurrection. To follow Jesus means to accept the cross, to walk with him against imperial violence and religious collaboration, and to pass through death to resurrection. Nothing is said about Jesus's doing it alone to excuse everyone else from having to follow him, and we emphasize that point pending subsequent discussion below.

You may recall that Mark does not detail the three great inaugural temptations of Jesus as Matthew and Luke do. In the third one (Matt. 4:8–10; Luke 4:5–8), Satan offers Jesus the entire world if he will but worship him. This offer reminds us that it is possible to gain control of the earth by demonic collaboration. It is possible to fall prey to the ancient (and modern) delusion of religious power backed by imperial violence. But Jesus personally refuses that temptation there, and Mark warns everyone against it here. This is, in one sense, Mark's version of that temptation— but, once again, it is not just for Jesus, but for all.

SECOND PROPHECY, REACTION, AND RESPONSE

This is the second of those three prophecies of his death and resurrection given to his disciples by the Markan Jesus in order to emphasize both his foreknowledge and their failure:

> They went on from there and passed through Galilee. He is not want anyone to know it; for he was teaching his disciples, saying to them, "The Son of Man is to be betrayed into human hands, and they will kill him, and three days after being killed, he will rise again." (9:30–31)

Mark has Jesus pass southward through Galilee without any distraction in order to concentrate completely on the disciples. And this time, those who would kill Jesus are mentioned only as

"human hands," but "death" is mentioned twice. Does Jesus suc-
ceed with the disciples this time?

No, because Mark continues with this extraordinary—in context—exchange:

> Then they came to Capernaum; and when he was in the
> house he asked them, "What were you arguing about on the
> way?" But they were silent, for on the way they had argued
> with one another who was the greatest. He sat down, called
> the twelve, and said to them, "Whoever wants to be first
> must be last of all and servant of all." (9:33–35)

Even as Jesus is announcing his death by execution, they are debating precedence among themselves. Here Mark is not only crit-
icizing the disciples; he is almost lampooning them. And, as we
see in the next instance, they completely ignore Jesus's admoni-
tion about becoming the first of all by being the servant of all, and
he has to say it all over again.

THIRD PROPHECY, REACTION, AND RESPONSE

This is the final, climactic, and most detailed of Mark's three
prophecies. It also continues what we have called the Lenten
journey theme as Jesus tries in vain not just to foretell but to explain his destiny to the disciples, so that they will be enabled to
follow him *on the way* through death to resurrected life. And once
again, and climactically, they are going to fail dismally in their response. Here, first of all, is the text:

> They were on the road, going up to Jerusalem, and Jesus
> was walking ahead of them; they were amazed, and those
> who followed were afraid. He took the twelve aside again
> and began to tell them what was to happen to him, saying,

"See, we are going up to Jerusalem, and the Son of Man will be handed over to the chief priests and the scribes, and they will condemn him to death; then they will hand him over to the Gentiles; they will mock him, and spit upon him, and flog him, and kill him; and after three days he will rise again." (10:32–34)

Notice that rather strange opening. It continues, of course, the journey theme that is represented by movement from Caesarea Philippi through Galilee to Jerusalem. Remember that the Greek word translated "road" (*hodos*) can also be translated by the more symbolically open "way"—they are all *on the way*, or at least supposed to be *on the way*, to death and resurrection.

Next, recall how Mark had opened the challenge of following Jesus to everyone ("the crowd") and not just to the twelve disciples after the first of the three prophecies in 8:34. This theme is repeated here and not too subtly. Jesus is "walking ahead" and "those who followed were afraid." That is the proper response, since Jesus has challenged them to follow him to death and resurrection. When, then, Jesus "took the twelve aside," Mark emphasizes again that they are not the only ones involved on this journey.

Furthermore, that third prophecy is the most detailed of the three. Mark 10:33–34 is in fact an outline of the later Markan account of Jesus's execution:

1. "handed over to the chief priests and the scribes"
   "Then Judas Iscariot, who was one of the twelve, went to the chief priests in order to betray [literally, hand over] him to them. When they heard it, they were greatly pleased, and promised to give him money. So he began to look for an opportunity to betray [literally, hand over] him." (14:10–11)

2. "and they will condemn him to death"
   "Then the high priest tore his clothes and said, 'Why do we still need witnesses? You have heard his blasphemy! What is your decision?' All of them condemned him as deserving death." (14:63–64)

3. "then they will hand him over to the Gentiles"
   "As soon as it was morning, the chief priests held a consultation with the elders and scribes and the whole council. They bound Jesus, led him away, and handed him over to Pilate." (15:1)

4. "they will mock him"
   "After mocking him, they stripped him of the purple cloak and put his own clothes on him." (15:20)

5. "and spit upon him"
   "They struck his head with a reed, spat upon him, and knelt down in homage to him." (15:19)

6. "and flog him"
   "So Pilate, wishing to satisfy the crowd, released Barabbas for them; and after flogging Jesus, he handed him over to be crucified." (15:15)

7. "and kill him"
   "And they crucified him, and divided his clothes among them, casting lots to decide what each should take." (15:24)

8. "and after three days he will rise again"
   "But he [the young man in the tomb] said to them [the women], 'Do not be alarmed; you are looking for Jesus of Nazareth, who was crucified. He has been raised; he is not here. Look, there is the place they laid him.'" (16:6)

Those correspondences emphasize for Mark that Jesus knows exactly and accepts completely what will happen in Jerusalem. But those three prophecies emphasize also that Jesus is calling *all* his followers—and not just the twelve disciples—to accept that communal destiny of death and resurrection. And, of course, as we have already seen in discussing the two symbolic demonstrations on Sunday and Monday of that last week, that confrontation is with oppressive foreign empire (against violence) and its collaborative local religion (against injustice), that is to say, with *any* religio-political combination that establishes injustice on an earth that belongs to a God of justice.

Finally, after each prophecy, however, Mark reports an absolute failure by the twelve disciples, and these failures are as repetitively significant as Jesus's prophecies. Here is what happens this time:

> James and John, the sons of Zebedee, came forward to him and said to him, "Teacher, we want you to do for us whatever we ask of you." And he said to them, "What is it you want me to do for you?" And they said to him, "Grant us to sit, one at your right hand and one at your left, in your glory." But Jesus said to them, "You do not know what you are asking. Are you able to drink the cup that I drink, or be baptized with the baptism that I am baptized with?" They replied, "We are able." Then Jesus said to them, "The cup that I drink you will drink; and with the baptism with which I am baptized, you will be baptized; but to sit at my right hand or at my left is not mine to grant, but it is for those for whom it has been prepared." (10:35–40)

That is only the first half of this third reaction and response. It continues into the second half with 10:41–45 and we return to that section below.

James and John skip easily over Jesus's death to concentrate on Jesus's glory and their own future participation in it. But, although the reaction to Jesus's third prophecy begins with James and John, it then expands to the rest of the twelve disciples. It is a parallel piece to the reaction to the first prophecy, which began with Peter and then expanded to the other disciples in 8:33. But notice that in the first prophecy's reaction and response Jesus was challenging them to die or at least be ready to die with him in Jerusalem. In the second and third ones, however, the emphasis is on how to behave—and behave as leaders—both now and hereafter.

The function of the three responses is to spell out in some detail what Jesus's destiny of execution and resurrection means for himself, for the Twelve, and for all his followers. We put here the second response and third response of Jesus in parallel columns to indicate how the latter text expands on the former:

MARK 9:35–37	MARK 10:42–45
Jesus sat down, called the twelve, and said to them, *"Whoever wants to be first must be last of all and servant of all"* Then he took a little child and put it among them; and taking it in his arms, he said to them, "Whoever welcomes one such child in my name welcomes me, and whoever welcomes me welcomes not me but the one who sent me."	Jesus called them and said to them, "You know that among the Gentiles those whom they recognize as their rulers lord it over them, and their great ones are tyrants over them. But it is not so among you; but *whoever wishes to become great among you must be your servant, and whoever wishes to be first among you must be slave of all.* For the Son of Man came not to be served but to serve, and to give his life a ransom for many."

What the disciples' participation entails is spelled out clearly in these twin responses. Even if, *physically*, they do not pass through death to resurrection alongside Jesus in Jerusalem and thereby end their lives on this earth, *metaphorically* their through-death-to-resurrection mode of existence will be one of paradoxical leadership in their continuing lives here below. They are called to lead like a child, a servant, a slave. It is at this point that Mark's unrelenting criticism of Peter, James and John, and the Twelve becomes most transparent. They act like the lords, rulers, and tyrants of the gentile world, and it is precisely against that world of domination that Jesus will demonstrate in Jerusalem.

ATONEMENT: SUBSTITUTION OR PARTICIPATION?

It is probably fair to say that *substitutionary atonement* is the only way that many or even most contemporary Christians understand faith in the sacrificial and salvific death of Jesus. That theological interpretation asserts that: (1) God has been deeply offended and dishonored by human sin; but (2) no amount of finite human punishment can atone for that infinite divine offense; so (3) God sent his own Divine Son to accept death as punishment for our sins in our place; and therefore (4) God's forgiveness is now freely available for all repentant sinners. It is not just that Jesus offered his life in atonement for sin, but that God demanded it as a condition for our forgiveness.

The basic and controlling metaphor for that understanding of God's design is our own experience of a responsible human judge who, no matter how loving, cannot legitimately or validly walk into her courtroom and clear the docket of all offenders by anticipatory forgiveness. The doctrine of vicarious, or substitutionary, atonement begs, of course, the question of whether God must or should be seen as a human judge writ large and absolute. That is surely not the only and maybe not the best metaphor for God. What about the metaphor, for example, in which God is fundamentally Parent (Father, if you prefer) rather than Judge? As such, and indeed as the Bible repeatedly asserts, God's unpunishing forgiveness has always been, is now, and ever will be freely available to any repentant sinner at any place at any time.

But how then do you move beyond forgiveness to establish a positive union with God as loving Parent? Since Jesus is for Christians the revelation, the image, and the best vision possible of that God, it is only by participation in the life, death, and resurrection of Jesus that such a salvific "at-one-ment" is possible.

Go back now and read once again those three prophecies, reactions, and responses in Mark 8:31–9:1, 9:31–37, and 10:33–45 in light of that choice between God as Judge or as Parent, that choice between substitution by Jesus for us or participation by us in Jesus. Notice, above all, how repeatedly Mark has Jesus insist that Peter, James and John, the Twelve, and all his followers on the way from Caesarea Philippi to Jerusalem must pass with him through death to a resurrected life whose content and style was spelled out relentlessly against their refusals to accept it. For Mark, it is about participation with Jesus and not substitution by Jesus. Mark has those followers recognize enough of that challenge that they change the subject and avoid the issue every time. To be fair to them, however, they still stay with Jesus. And every year, our Lent asks us to repent, change, and participate in that transition with Jesus. But to do so, as we know, would be to negate the normalcy of civilization's lust for domination and to deny the legitimacy of what lords and kings have always been and what nations and empires have always done.

But wait a minute. What about that climactic conclusion in Mark 10:45, which states that "the Son of Man came not to be served but to serve, and to give his life a ransom for many"? Does that metaphor of "ransom," or redemption, not indicate substitutionary atonement? Possibly, if taken as an isolated saying, but certainly not in its Markan context of the journey from Caesarea Philippi to Jerusalem.

The Greek word translated "ransom" is *lutron*, which means the payment to an owner for a slave's freedom or a captive's ransom. It is not used in the Greek of the Hebrew Bible for anything like vicarious satisfaction or vicarious atonement to God for sin. A typical usage is in connection with Cyrus, the sixth-century Persian emperor who, after conquering Babylon, freed and sent home those Jews taken into captivity by the Babylonians. And Cyrus would not even demand any ransom for their redemption, according to Isaiah:

> I have aroused Cyrus in righteousness, and I will make all his paths straight; he shall build my city and set my exiles free, not for price or reward, says the Lord of hosts. (45:13)

In that text from Isaiah, the Greek word for "price" is *lutron*, or "ransom." Cyrus will not only free them; he will not demand any ransom in return.

How does Mark think Jesus's death is a "ransom" (*lutron*) for many? The Markan Jesus has been insisting on the "how" ever since Caesarea Philippi—to the Twelve in particular but also to all others as well. It is not by Jesus *substituting* for them, but by their *participating* in Jesus. They must pass through death to a new life here below upon this earth, and they can already see what that transformed life is like in Jesus himself.

IN REMEMBRANCE OF HER

Mark's relentless criticism of Peter, of James and John, of the Twelve, and especially of Judas was a necessary preparation for answering one very important question concerning the incident in 14:3–9. That story opens with this action by an unnamed woman: "While he was at Bethany in the house of Simon the leper, as he sat at the table, a woman came with an alabaster jar of very costly ointment of nard, and she broke open the jar and poured the ointment on his head" (14:3). The account continues by emphasizing the very great value of the ointment; it "could have been sold for more than three hundred denarii, and the money given to the poor" (14:5). To use ointment worth a year's wages for a laborer was certainly kind and generous even to the point of extravagance and certainly was "a good service" for Jesus (14:6). But why does she deserve or her action receive this absolutely unique and stunningly extraordinary accolade from Jesus: "Truly I tell you, wherever the good news is proclaimed in the whole world, what she has done will be told in remembrance of her" (14:9).

When the preceding verse is read against that continuous criticism of the Twelve just noted, the significance of her action becomes clear. "She has done what she could," says Jesus, "she has anointed my body beforehand for its burial" (14:8). She alone, of all those who heard Jesus's three prophecies of his death and resurrection, believed him and drew the obvious conclusion. *Since* (not if) *you are going to die and rise, I must anoint you now beforehand, because I will never have a chance to do it afterward.* She is, for Mark, the first believer. She is, for us, the first Christian. And she believed from the word of Jesus before any discovery of an empty tomb.

Furthermore, her action was a graphic demonstration of the paradoxical leadership cited by Jesus for himself and all his followers on the model of child, servant, and slave. Recall those parallel texts from Jesus's second and third responses given above. They serve as preparation for this scene. *The unnamed woman is not only the first believer; she is also the model leader.*

Jesus has been telling the Twelve what leadership entails from Caesarea Philippi to Jerusalem and has gotten nowhere with them. But this unnamed woman believed him and, presumably,

Mark locates her among those others beside the Twelve who have been accompanying him *on the way*. "There were also women looking on from a distance; among them were Mary Magdalene, and Mary the mother of James the younger and of Joses, and Salome. These used to follow him and provided for him when he was in Galilee; and there were many other women who had come up with him to Jerusalem" (15:40–41). She was both one of those "many other women" and the first and only one who believed what Jesus had been telling them repeatedly. Hence that supreme and unique praise for her as the first believer and the model leader. Mark's intercalation, or frame, is also now clear. The unnamed woman represents the perfect disciple-leader and is contrasted with Judas, who represents the worst one possible.

It is also very important, by the way, not to confuse that story in Mark 11:3–9 about the woman who anointed Jesus "in the house of Simon the leper" in Judea with the other story in Luke 7:36–50 about the woman who anointed Jesus "in the Pharisee's house" in Galilee. That is a different story—different in place, time, and meaning. But, for Mark, that unnamed woman is, in our terms, the first Christian, and she believed, again in our terms, even before the first Easter.

THE MOTIVE OF JUDAS

Mark gives absolutely no hint of Judas's motive in betraying Jesus. He simply records it along with this response from the chief priests: "When they heard it, they were greatly pleased, and promised to give him money" (14:11). Mark, by the way, does not say that Judas did it for money, simply that they promised him some.

The other gospels, however, let alone later Christian imagination, were not content to leave the story there. Matthew retells Mark 14:11 by saying that, when Judas went to the high priests, he asked them, "What will you give me if I betray him to you?" They paid him thirty pieces of silver (16:15). And, since he did it for money, they had to pay up front. That allows Matthew to conclude the story of Judas in 27:3–10 and to connect that sum of "thirty pieces of silver" with Zechariah 11:12.

John goes even further in explaining Judas's motivation. On a theological level, according to John, he was either a devil or at least under diabolical influence. But Jesus always knew what Judas would do: "'Did I not choose you, the twelve? Yet one of you is a devil.' He was speaking of Judas son of Simon Iscariot, for he, though one of the twelve, was going to betray him" (6:70–71). Next, during that unnamed woman's anointing at Bethany, the protest does not come from a vague "some" as in Mark 14:4, but specifically from "Judas Iscariot, one of his disciples (the one who was about to betray him)" (12:4). And John explains his protest with this parenthetical comment: "He said this not because he cared about the poor, but because he was a thief; he kept the common purse and used to steal what was put into it" (12:6). Finally, on the night of Jesus's arrest, John mentions the devil twice in connection with Judas: "The devil had already put it into the heart of Judas son of Simon Iscariot to betray him" (13:2); "After he received the piece of bread, Satan entered into him. Jesus said to him, 'Do quickly what you are going to do'" (13:27).

All of that is simply standard imagination: Judas did it for money; Judas did it because he was a thief, and so forth. Scholars and novelists have added several other reasons. For example, Judas had become convinced that nonviolent resistance would not work and was ultimately foolish. Or, again, he became afraid that he would be arrested with Jesus and the best solution was to betray Jesus and save himself. But Mark's emphasis is not on Judas's motive, whatever it was, but on Judas's membership in the Twelve. Notice how he uses it almost like a title every time he mentions Judas after 3:19 (14:10, 43). He is always "Judas-one-of-the-Twelve" just in case we might ever forget it. Judas's identity among the Twelve, not Judas's motive for betraying Jesus, is Mark's emphasis. His betrayal is simply the worst example of how those closest to Jesus failed him dismally in Jerusalem. The traitor has entered into an agreement with those who collaborate with imperial rule. And so Wednesday ends and the plot has been set in motion.

—·◆·—

FIVE

THURSDAY

On the first day of Unleavened Bread, when the Passover lamb is sacrificed, his disciples said to him, "Where do you want us to go and make the preparations for you to eat the Passover?" So he sent two of his disciples, saying to them, "Go into the city, and a man carrying a jar of water will meet you; follow him, and wherever he enters, say to the owner of the house, 'The Teacher asks, Where is my guest room where I may eat the Passover with my disciples?' He will show you a large room upstairs, furnished and ready. Make preparations for us there." So the disciples set out and went to the city, and found everything as he had told them; and they prepared the Passover meal.

MARK 14:12–16

—·◆·—

Mark's story of Jesus's last week moves toward its climax. On Wednesday Jesus had been anointed for burial by an unnamed woman follower and betrayed to the authorities by one of the twelve men closest to him. On Thursday, the events set in motion by Wednesday unfold. For most Christians, the liturgical observance of "Maundy Thursday," as it is commonly known, begins the most solemn part of the most sacred week of the Christian year. Along with Palm Sunday, Good Friday, and Easter, it is the best-known day of Holy Week.

Holy Thursday is full of drama. In the evening, Jesus eats a final meal with his followers and prays for deliverance in Gethsemane; he is betrayed by Judas, denied by Peter, and abandoned by the rest of his disciples. Arrested in the darkness, he is then interrogated and condemned to death by the high priest and his council, the local collaborators with imperial authority. All of this happens before daybreak on Friday. And because we are following the time indicators in Mark's narrative, our treatment of Friday in the next chapter will begin "at dawn," when Jesus is transferred from the custody of the temple authorities to the imperial governor.

Before we turn to Mark's story of Thursday, we note how different it is from the story of this day in John's gospel. First, the dating is different. In Mark (followed by Matthew and Luke), the meal Jesus shares with his disciples is a Passover meal. In John, it is not. Rather, Thursday is the day before Passover, and the lambs to be eaten at the Passover meal on Friday evening will be killed on Friday afternoon, at about the same hour that Jesus dies on the cross. The reason for John's dating seems to be theological: Jesus is the new Passover lamb. Second, the amount of space devoted to Jesus's last gathering with his disciples is very different: in Mark, nine verses (14:17–25); in John, five chapters (13–17), often called "Jesus's Farewell Discourse."

Third, what happens at this gathering is also very different. In Mark (again followed by Matthew and Luke), Jesus speaks the words that, in slightly varying forms, have become central to Christian celebration of the Lord's Supper (Eucharist, Mass, or Communion): "This is my body, this is my blood." John says nothing about this. Instead, John has the story of Jesus washing the feet of his disciples (13:3–11), a ritual often incorporated into Christian observance of Holy Thursday. Finally, we note that calling this day "Maundy Thursday" is based on John's story: "Maundy" derives from the Latin word for the "mandate"—the new commandment—that Jesus gives his followers in John 13:34: "I give you a new commandment, that you love one another. Just as I have loved you, you also should love one another." Of course, these differences do not mean that John should be disregarded in Maundy Thursday services. It is simply that these features of John's account are not part of Mark's story of Thursday.

Mark's overture to Thursday is the preparation for the Passover meal to be eaten in the evening (14:12–16). Jesus tells two of his disciples to go into the city, where they will be met by a "man carrying a jar of water." They are to ask him for and follow him to a guest room where the "Teacher" may eat the Passover meal with his disciples. The disciples follow Jesus's instructions, find the room, and make preparations there for the Passover meal.

Details in this passage recall the preparations for Jesus's entry into the city on Palm Sunday. In both cases, Jesus sends two of his disciples, tells them what to look for, and instructs them what to say. In the first case, the preplanning was for a public demonstration, an anti-imperial entrance affirming nonviolence that countered the violence-based triumphal entrance of imperial power, namely, of Pilate, for Passover crowd control.

In the second case, the preplanning has to do with secrecy. The overture to Thursday follows the verse announcing that Judas "began to look for an opportunity to betray him" (14:11). By reporting that Jesus sent *two* disciples to make clandestine arrangements for the Passover meal, Mark has Jesus withhold from Judas its precise location, so that Judas cannot tell the authorities where to find Jesus during the meal. This meal—what we shall call the New Passover—matters, and Judas must not be allowed to interfere with its completion.[10]

As Mark tells the story, Jesus knows what will happen. We need not attribute this to supernatural foreknowledge. Jesus must have known that the noose was tightening, that the cross was approaching. He could not have been oblivious to the hostility of the authorities, and he may well have regarded his arrest and execution as inevitable—not because of divine necessity, but because of what he could see happening around him.

THE LAST SUPPER: A WEB OF MEANINGS

When it was evening, he came with the twelve. And when they had taken their places and were eating, Jesus said, "Truly I tell you, one of you will betray me, one who is eating with me." They began to be distressed and to say to him one after another, "Surely, not I?" He said to them, "It is one of the twelve, one who is dipping bread into the bowl with me. For the Son of Man goes as it is written of him, but woe to that one by whom the Son of Man is betrayed! It would have been better for that one not to have been born."

While they were eating, he took a loaf of bread, and after blessing it he broke it, gave it to them, and said, "Take; this is my body." Then he took a cup, and after giving thanks he gave it to them, and all of them drank from it. He said to them, "This is my blood of the covenant, which is poured out for many. Truly I tell you, I will never again drink of the fruit of the vine until that day when I drink it new in the kingdom of God."

MARK 14:17–25

———◆———

With the arrival of evening, Jesus and all twelve disciples, including Judas, come to the upstairs room where the arrangements have been made. There are three main elements in Mark's story of the Last Supper: they eat the Passover meal together; Jesus speaks of his imminent betrayal; and then Jesus invests the bread and wine with meanings associated with his impending death.

We begin with the middle element of the three, Jesus's disclosure that he knows he will be betrayed. While they were eating Jesus says: "Truly I tell you, one of you will betray me, one who is eating with me. . . . It is one of the twelve. . . . For the Son of Man goes as it is written of him, but woe to that one by whom the Son of Man is betrayed! It would have been better for that one not to have been born" (14:18–21). Indeed, before the night is over, Jesus will not only have been betrayed by Judas, but denied by Peter and abandoned by the rest. The theme of failed discipleship continues to be central; more than half of Mark's narration of Thursday evening and night is devoted to it (thirty-three of sixty-one verses: 14:18–21, 27–45, 50–52, 66–72).

In the course of the Passover meal, Jesus shares a loaf of bread and a cup of wine with his disciples and speaks the words, often called the "words of institution," that became the core of the Christian Eucharist: "He took a loaf of bread, and after blessing it he broke it, gave it to them, and said, *'Take; this is my body.'* Then he took a cup, and after giving thanks he gave it to them, and all of them drank from it. He said to them, *'This is my blood of the covenant, which is poured out for many.'*"

This final meal that Jesus shared with his disciples has multiple resonances of meaning. It connects backward into the public activity of Jesus and forward into his death and the post-Easter life of Christianity. Jesus's Last Supper was to be the First Supper of the future. We will highlight four of its rich meanings.

A Continuation of the Meal Practice of Jesus

According to the gospels, including Mark, shared meals were one of the most distinctive features of Jesus's public activity. He often taught at meals, banquets were topics of his parables, and his meal practice was often criticized by his opponents. Scribes and Pharisees aggressively ask, "Why does he eat with tax collectors and sinners?" (Mark 2:16; see also Matt. 11:19; Luke 7:34; 15:1–2). The issue is that Jesus eats with "undesirables," the marginalized and outcast, in a society in which the people with whom one shared a meal was hugely significant. Jesus's meal practice was about inclusion in a society with sharp social boundaries. It had both religious and political significance: religious because it was done in the name of the kingdom of God; political because it affirmed a very different vision of society. An analogy close to our own time would be a religious leader in the American South prior to the antisegregation legislation of the 1960s holding public integrated meals and declaring, "*This* is the kingdom of God—and the divided world that you see around you is not."

But meals were not just about inclusion. They were also, and crucially, about food. The meals of Jesus were not ritual meals in which food had only or primarily symbolic meaning. They were real meals, not a morsel and a sip as in our observance of the Eucharist. For Jesus, real food—bread—mattered. In his teaching, "bread" symbolized the material basis of existence, as in the Lord's Prayer, or the "Our Father." Immediately after the petition, "Your kingdom come, your will be done on earth, as it is in heaven," is "Give us this day our daily bread." For Jesus's peasant audience, bread—enough food for the day—was one of the two central survival issues of their lives (the other was debt). The Last Supper continues and culminates in Jesus's emphasis upon meals and food as God's justice.

An Echo of the Feeding of the Five Thousand

As Mark narrates what Jesus did at the Last Supper, he uses four verbs: *took, blessed, broke,* and *gave.* These four key words refer us back to an earlier scene concerning food in Mark, in which Jesus feeds five thousand people with a few loaves and fishes: "*Taking* the five loaves and the two fish, Jesus looked up to heaven, and *blessed* and *broke* the loaves, and *gave* them to his disciples to set before the people; and he divided the two fish among them all" (6:41). Why this cross-reference from the Last Supper back to the loaves-and-fishes meal?

Mark's story of the multiplication of the loaves and fishes begins by establishing two divergent solutions to a hunger situation. People (five thousand, Mark says) have listened to Jesus all day in a deserted place, it is now late, and they are hungry. The solution from the disciples is quite reasonable: "*Send them away* so that they may go into the surrounding country and villages and buy something for themselves to eat" (6:36). The alternate solution from Jesus seems quite impossible, "*You give them* something to eat" (6:37), to which the disciples respond. "Are we to go and buy two hundred denarii worth of bread, and give it to them to eat?" This difference between Jesus and his disciples is established, yet as the story proceeds Jesus forces them to participate step by step as intermediaries in the entire process. Jesus has them find what food is available (6:38), make the people sit down in groups (6:39), distribute the food (6:41), and pick up what is left over afterward (6:43). In other words, they are forced to accept and participate in Jesus's solution (*give them food*) and not in their own (*send them away*).

Note that Jesus does not bring down manna from heaven or turn stones into food. He takes what is already there, the five loaves and two fishes, and, when it passes through *Jesus's* hands, there is more than enough, much more than enough, for everyone present. The point of this story is not multiplication, but distribution. The food already there is enough for all when it passes through the hands of Jesus as the incarnation of divine justice. The disciples—think of them as the *already present* kingdom community in microcosm, or as the leaders of that community— do not see that as their responsibility and are forced to accept it by Jesus. Behind that, of course, is an entire theology of creation in which God owns the world, demands that all get a fair share of its goods, and appoints humans as stewards to establish God's justice on earth.

Mark's emphasis on a just distribution of what does not belong to us in the incident of the loaves and fishes links, therefore, to the emphasis on the "loaf of bread" and the "cup of wine" that are shared among all at the New Passover meal. Once again, Jesus distributes food already present to "all" who are there. A shared meal of what is already there among all those present becomes *both* the great sacramental symbol *and* the primary practical program of the kingdom movement.

A Passover Meal

As a Passover meal, Jesus's Last Supper resonates with the story of the exodus from Egypt, his people's story of their birth as a nation. A story of bondage, deliverance, and liberation, it was their primordial narrative, the most important story they knew. Passover was (and is) the great annual Jewish celebration of God's greatest act of deliverance.

The first Passover (Exod. 12) occurred on the evening before the tenth plague to strike Pharaoh and Egypt, namely, the death of the firstborn in every household in Egypt. That plague was the hammer that broke Pharaoh's will, and the Hebrew slaves were finally liberated. In this narrative context, the Passover lamb had two primary meanings. First, some of the blood from the Passover lamb was to be put on the doorposts of the houses of the Hebrew slaves so that the angel of death, "the destroyer," would pass over those houses and not kill the firstborn in them:

> They shall take some of the blood and put it on the two doorposts and the lintel of the houses in which they eat it. . . . For the Lord will pass through to strike down the Egyptians; when he sees the blood on the lintel and on the two doorposts, the Lord will pass over that door and will not allow the destroyer to enter your houses to strike you down. (12:7, 23)

Second, each family was then to eat their Passover lamb, gird their loins, put on their sandals, and be ready to leave. The Passover lamb was thus also food for the journey. Moreover the first Passover was also the last supper in Egypt, the land of bondage.

We note that the Passover lamb is a sacrifice in the broad sense of the word, but not in the narrow sense of substitutionary sacrifice. Its purpose is twofold: protection against death and food for the journey. The story makes no mention of sin or guilt, substitution or atonement.

The Passover meal, the *seder*, memorializes the first Passover and the exodus by bringing it into the present. The elements of the meal embody central elements in the story, and the words make clear that the story is not simply about the past, but is also about the present: "It was not only our fathers and mothers who were Pharaoh's slaves in Egypt, but we, all of us gathered here tonight, were Pharaoh's slaves in Egypt; and it was not only our fathers and mothers who were liberated by the great and mighty hand of God, but all of us here have been liberated by God." For the empire of Pharaoh, substitute the Roman Empire or any other empire, and the subversive nature of this story is not difficult to discern.

Body and Blood and the Death of Jesus

Mark's story of the Last Supper leaves the connections to Passover implicit. What it makes explicit is the connection to Jesus's impending death. It does so with the "words of institution," familiar to Christians because of their use in the Lord's Supper:

> He took a loaf of bread, and after blessing it he broke it, gave it to them, and said, "*Take; this is my body.*" Then he took a cup, and after giving thanks he gave it to them, and all of them drank from it. He said to them, "*This is my blood of the covenant, which is poured out for many.*" (14:22–24)

In Matthew, Luke, and Paul the italicized words spoken over the bread and cup appear in slightly different form (and they are not in John at all). In Matthew, the words over the bread are almost identical to Mark's: "Take, eat; this is my body" (26:26). The words over the cup are extended and connected to forgiveness: "Drink from it, all of you; for this is my blood of the covenant, which is poured out for many for the forgiveness of sins" (26:27–28). Luke's version of what is said over the bread differs more. He adds "given for you" and the theme of "remembrance": "This is my body, which is given for you. Do this in remembrance of me" (22:19). Over the cup, Luke has, "This cup that is poured out for you is the new covenant in my blood" (22:20). Paul's account, written earlier than any of the gospels, has the remembrance theme in both parts, and is closest to Luke: "This [bread] is my body that is for you. Do this in remembrance of me. . . . This cup is the new covenant in my blood. Do this, as often as you drink it, in remembrance of me" (1 Cor. 11:24–25).

The different versions indicate a degree of fluidity in how the Last Supper was remembered and celebrated. What they all have in common, however, is an emphasis on body and blood, bread and wine. Whatever connections Mark intended from the loaves-and-fishes meal to this bread-and-wine meal, there was nothing in that earlier meal that spoke of body-and-blood symbolism. What, then, is Mark adding here that was not present before?

First, the point of Jesus's meals—from the loaves-and-fishes ones to the bread-and-wine one—is to insist on shared meals as the mandate of divine justice in a world not our own. If, as God asserts in Leviticus 25:23, "The land is mine; with me you are but aliens and tenants," then of course the food the land produces belongs likewise to God. If we are all tenant farmers and resident aliens on an *earth* not our own, then we are also invitees and guests at a table not our own. But if one lives for divine justice in a world that belongs to God, one will usually die a violent death from human injustice in a world that refuses recognition of such ownership.

The language of body and blood points to a violent death. When a person dies nonviolently we speak of a separation of body and soul. But when a person dies violently we speak of a separation of body and blood. That is the first and basic point of Jesus's *separated* bread/body and wine/blood words. He does not simply take bread and wine together and say, "This is my body and blood."

Second, that separation of Jesus's body and blood by violent death is the absolutely necessary basis for another level of meaning in Mark. It would never have been possible to speak of Jesus's death as a blood sacrifice unless, first, it had been a violent execution. But, granted that fate, a correlation becomes possible between Jesus as the new paschal lamb and this final meal as a New Passover. Recall what was said about the ancient (and modern) understanding of sacrifice in Chapter 2. The point is neither suffering nor substitution, but participation with God through gift or meal.

Earlier, in Mark 10:45, Jesus said that "the Son of Man came not to be served but to serve, and to give his life a ransom for many." That liberation or redemption or salvation is echoed here in Jesus's statement that "This is my blood of the covenant, which is poured out for many" (14:24). But neither verse explains how exactly that blood or ransom effects its liberation "for many." Recall, however, the challenge of Jesus in 8:34–35: "He called the crowd with his disciples, and said to them, 'If any want to become my followers, let them deny themselves and take up their cross and follow me. For those who want to save their life will lose it, and those who lose their life for my sake, and for the sake of the gospel, will save it.'" Recall also the reactions and responses from the Twelve to Jesus's three prophecies. Peter wanted no part of that fate, the Twelve debated their relative worth, and James and John wanted first seats afterward. But Jesus had explained to them quite clearly that his and their life was a flat contradiction to the normalcy of civilization's domination systems. In other words, it was by participation *with* Jesus and, even more, *in* Jesus that his followers were to pass through death to resurrection, from the domination life of human normalcy to the servant life of human transcendence.

Finally, Jesus does not merely speak of bread and wine as symbols of his body and blood. Rather, he has all of the Twelve (including Judas!) actually partake of the food and drink—they all participate in the bread-as-body and blood-as-wine. It is, as it were, a final attempt to bring all of them with him through execution to resurrection, through death to new life. It is, once again, about *participation* in Christ and not *substitution* by Christ. And we, like they, are invited to travel with Jesus through execution to resurrection. The Last Supper is about bread for the world, God's justice against human injustice, a New Passover from bondage to liberation, and participation in the path that leads through death to new life.

GETHSEMANE, PRAYER, AND ARREST

When they had sung the hymn, they went out to the Mount of Olives. And Jesus said to them, "You will all become deserters; for it is written, 'I will strike the shepherd, and the sheep will be scattered.' But after I am raised up, I will go before you to Galilee." Peter said to him, "Even though all become deserters, I will not." Jesus said to him, "Truly I tell you, this day, this very night, before the cock crows twice, you will deny me three times." But he said vehemently, "Even though I must die with you, I will not deny you." And all of them said the same.

They went to a place called Gethsemane; and he said to his disciples, "Sit here while I pray." He took with him Peter and James and John, and began to be distressed and agitated. And he said to them, "I am deeply grieved, even to death; remain here, and keep awake." And going a little farther, he threw himself on the ground and prayed that, if it were possible, the hour might pass from him. He said, "Abba, Father, for you all things are possible; remove this

cup from me; yet, not what I want, but what you want."
He came and found them sleeping; and he said to Peter,
"Simon, are you asleep? Could you not keep awake one
hour? Keep awake and pray that you may not come into the
time of trial; the spirit indeed is willing, but the flesh is
weak." And again he went away and prayed, saying the same
words. And once more he came and found them sleeping,
for their eyes were very heavy; and they did not know what
to say to him. He came a third time and said to them, "Are
you still sleeping and taking your rest? Enough! The hour
has come; the Son of Man is betrayed into the hands of sinners. Get up, let us be going. See, my betrayer is at hand."

Immediately, while he was still speaking, Judas, one of
the twelve, arrived; and with him there was a crowd with
swords and clubs, from the chief priests, the scribes, and the
elders. Now the betrayer had given them a sign, saying,
"The one I will kiss is the man; arrest him and lead him
away under guard." So when he came, he went up to him at
once and said, "Rabbi!" and kissed him. Then they laid
hands on him and arrested him. But one of those who stood
near drew his sword and struck the slave of the high priest,
cutting off his ear. Then Jesus said to them, "Have you come
out with swords and clubs to arrest me as though I were a
bandit? Day after day I was with you in the temple teaching,
and you did not arrest me. But let the scriptures be fulfilled." All of them deserted him and fled.

A certain young man was following him, wearing nothing but a linen cloth. They caught hold of him, but he left
the linen cloth and ran off.

MARK 14:26−52

————— • ◆ • —————

As the meal ends, Jesus and the disciples sing a hymn and de-
part from the upstairs room. They leave the city and go to an area

at the foot of the Mount of Olives known as Gethsemane, a hundred yards or so outside the east wall of the city. This is the longest section of Mark's account of Thursday (14:26–52, a total of twenty-seven verses). In it:

Jesus tells his disciples that they will all become deserters.

Peter vows that he will not desert Jesus, and Jesus tells him, "Before the cock crows twice, you will deny me three times."

Jesus tells the inner three of his disciples (Peter, James, and John) to stay awake while he prays. Three times they fall asleep, and each time they are reprimanded by Jesus.

Jesus prays for deliverance.

Judas arrives with a group of temple soldiers, and Jesus is arrested.

The disciples flee.

We will focus on Jesus's prayer and his arrest.

After Jesus and his disciples arrive in Gethsemane, Jesus goes a short distance away from them in order to pray, taking Peter and James and John with him. Mark's spare description of Jesus as "distressed," "agitated," "deeply grieved, even to death," and throwing himself upon the ground, is filled with anguish:

Jesus began to be distressed and agitated. And he said to them, "I am deeply grieved, even to death; remain here, and keep awake." And going a little farther, he threw himself on the ground and prayed that, if it were possible, the hour might pass from him. He said, "Abba, Father, for you all things are possible; remove this cup from me; yet, not what I want, but what you want." (14:33–36)

The prayer is remarkable both for its way of addressing God and its content.

Jesus calls God *abba,* an Aramaic word that Mark includes even though he is writing in Greek. In Aramaic, *abba* is the familiar or intimate form of "father," much like the English "papa." It was used by children to address their father not only as toddlers but also as adults. As a term for addressing God, it was very unusual but not unique in ancient Judaism. We know of a few Jewish figures near the time of Jesus who spoke of God as *abba.* They were known for their intimacy with God, their long hours of prayer, and their healing powers. The term suggests that Jesus (like them) felt an intimacy with God like that between child and parent.

Jesus prays for deliverance. He prays that this hour might pass from him, that this cup might be removed. Both "hour" and "cup" refer to his impending torture and cruel death. Not surprisingly, he would rather not go through it. Yet he hands himself over: "Yet, not what I want, but what you want." An older English translation is more familiar to many of us: "Yet not my will, but thy will be done." It is important to add that this does not mean that Jesus's death was the will of God. It is never God's will that the righteous suffer. It was not God's will that Jesus died, any more than it was the will of God that any of the martyrs before and after Jesus were killed. Yet we may imagine them handing themselves over in the way that Jesus did, from Peter and Paul to Thecla and Perpetua to Dietrich Bonhoeffer and the nuns in El Salvador. The prayer reflects not a fatalistic resignation to the will of God, but a trusting in God in the midst of the most dire of circumstances.

At some point after the Passover meal, Judas leaves the group (in John, he leaves during the meal; in Mark, Matthew, and Luke, he apparently remains throughout the meal). He knows where Jesus and the disciples are going and where Jesus can be arrested in the darkness away from the crowds. After Jesus's prayer:

Judas, one of the twelve, arrived; and with him there was a crowd with swords and clubs, from the chief priests, the scribes, and the elders. Now the betrayer had given them a sign, saying, "The one I will kiss is the man; arrest him and lead him away under guard." So when he came, he went up to him at once and said, "Rabbi!" and kissed him. Then they laid hands on him and arrested him. (14:43–46)

The "crowd with swords and clubs, from the chief priests, the scribes, and the elders" refers to a group of temple police or temple soldiers. As local collaborators, the temple authorities were permitted by the Romans to have a small military force, more than a police force but less than an army. John's gospel describes the arresting party very differently. Rather than being temple soldiers sent by the temple authorities (and probably a relatively small group), they are a group of six hundred imperial soldiers.

Judas identifies Jesus with a kiss. Readers of the gospels have sometimes wondered why this was necessary. Surely the authorities knew who Jesus was? But it is not the interrogators from earlier in the week, the chief priests and scribes, who come out to arrest him, but temple soldiers sent by them. It is easy to imagine that they would not have known which one Jesus was.

Then Mark reports, "One of those who stood near drew his sword and struck the slave of the high priest, cutting off his ear" (14:47). In Luke and John, the story grows. Luke reports that Jesus heals the man whose ear has been severed, the only gospel to do so (22:51). John reports that it was Peter who wielded the sword and names the slave as Malchus (18:10). The story is surprising, for it reports that one of Jesus's followers was armed. Was this standard practice among them? Or is this another instance of Mark's theme of failed discipleship? In any case, in both Matthew and Luke, Jesus disavows the action. In Matthew, he says, "Put your sword back into its place; for all who take the sword will perish by the sword" (26:52). In Luke, "No more of this!" (22:51).

It is instructive to compare Mark's story of the arrest with John's account. In Mark, Jesus is a vulnerable human being. In John, Jesus is in charge and is even acknowledged as a divine being by those who arrest him. To be specific:

- In Mark Jesus prays, "Remove this cup from me; yet, not what I want, but what you want" (14:36). Not so in John. Earlier in John, Jesus prayed, "Now my soul is troubled. And what should I say—'Father, save me from this hour'? No, it is for this reason that I have come to this hour" (12:27). In the garden of Gethsemane, he says, "Am I not to drink the cup that the Father has given me?" (18:11).

- In Mark, the disciples all flee. In John, Jesus orders the soldiers who are arresting him to let his disciples go, "Let these men go," followed by John's comment, "This was to fulfill the word that he had spoken, 'I did not lose a single one of those whom you gave me'" (18:8–9). That refers to 17:12, where Jesus said, speaking to God, "While I was with them, I protected them in your name that you have given me. I guarded them, and not one of them was lost except the one destined to be lost, so that the scripture might be fulfilled."

- In Mark 14:35 Jesus "threw himself on the ground." In John, when the six hundred imperial soldiers arrive to arrest Jesus, "Jesus asked them, 'Whom are you looking for?' They answered, 'Jesus of Nazareth.' Jesus replied, 'I am he.' Judas, who betrayed him, was standing with them. When Jesus said to them, 'I am he,' they stepped back and fell to the ground" (18:4–6).

  This is a remarkable story. Why do the soldiers—all six hundred of them—fall to the ground when Jesus says, "I am he"? Because "I am" is the sacred name of God in the Jewish Bible (Exod. 3:14). They fall down in the presence of the sacred—and then promptly arrest Jesus. Historically, it is impossible to imagine this scene: six hundred imperial soldiers acknowledging the presence of the sacred in Jesus, and then arresting him anyway. Theologically, it is an effective scene: even the empire that kills Jesus acknowledges his lordship—and tries to do away with it.

We conclude this section with the role of the disciples. We have already mentioned how central the theme of failed discipleship is to Mark's gospel and to Thursday in particular. Judas betrays Jesus, Peter denies him, and the rest flee. They now disappear from the story of Holy Week. Mark does not mention them again until Easter. In this he is followed by the other gospels, except that both Matthew and Luke tell us about the fate of Judas. According to Matthew 27:3–10, Judas returned to the chief priests and elders the thirty pieces of silver he had received for betraying Jesus, and then went out and committed suicide by hanging himself. According to Luke in Acts 1:18–19 (the same author wrote both Luke and Acts), Judas bought a field with the money, and then fell, burst open in the middle, and died as his bowels gushed out. Though Luke does not say that this was a judgment of God, clearly he intends it. In Matthew, Judas is a suicide; in Luke, he dies a horrible but not self-inflicted death.

But, with the exception of Judas, we do not hear of the disciples again until Easter. In the Easter stories—implicitly in Mark and explicitly in the other gospels—Peter and the rest of the disciples are restored to relationship and community by Jesus. Indeed, had Judas not killed himself or died suddenly, we may imagine that even the betrayer would have been restored to relationship and community.

INTERROGATION AND CONDEMNATION

They took Jesus to the high priest; and all the chief priests, the elders, and the scribes were assembled. Peter had followed him at a distance, right into the courtyard of the high priest; and he was sitting with the guards, warming himself at the fire. Now the chief priests and the whole council were looking for testimony against Jesus to put him to death; but they found none. For many gave false testimony against him, and their testimony did not agree. Some stood up and gave false testimony against him, saying, "We heard him say, 'I will destroy this temple that is made with hands, and in three days I will build another, not made with hands.'" But even on this point their testimony did not agree. Then the high priest stood up before them and asked Jesus, "Have you no answer? What is it that they testify against you?" But he was silent and did not answer. Again the high priest asked him, "Are you the Messiah, the Son of the Blessed One?" Jesus said, "I am; and 'you will see the Son of Man seated at the right hand of the Power,' and 'coming with the clouds of heaven.'" Then the high priest tore his clothes and said, "Why do we still need witnesses? You have heard his blasphemy! What is your decision?" All of them condemned him as deserving death. Some began to spit on him, to blindfold him, and to strike him, saying to him, "Prophesy!" The guards also took him over and beat him.

MARK 14:53–65

———— • ◆ • ————

Now Jesus is taken to the temple authorities, whom Mark names as "the high priest, and all the chief priests, the elders, and the scribes" (14:53) and as "the chief priests and the whole council" (14:55). What follows is often called "the Jewish trial of Jesus" before "the high priest" and "the whole council," resulting in Jesus's condemnation to death. As narrated in Mark and the other gospels, it has led most Christians throughout the centuries to assign primary responsibility for the death of Jesus to the highest-ranking members of the Jewish nation and thus, uncritically, to "the Jews." The story of Jesus's interrogation and condemnation by the high priest and his council has often become a text of terror for Jews in subsequent centuries.

Thus we need to pause for some historical comments. Though our purpose is to exposit Mark's story of Holy Week and not to reconstruct the history behind it, here it is important to do so and to emphasize:

- Most likely, Mark (and other early Christians) did not know exactly what happened. The reason is that, according to Mark (and the other gospels), no follower of Jesus was present with him subsequent to his arrest (they had all fled). Though it is possible to imagine that somebody within the high priest's circle later disclosed what happened, we cannot be at all certain of this. Thus the trial scene may represent a post-Easter Christian construction and not history remembered. We need to remember that this is the way Mark tells the story around the year 70.

- It is unclear whether we should think of Mark as presenting a formal "trial" or an informal but deadly "hearing." "Trial" implies a legal procedure that follows the accepted rules of the time; "hearing" implies a para-legal or even extra-legal procedure. Moreover, the "council" referred to by Mark may not have been the Sanhedrin of later centuries, but a "privy council" consisting of the high priest and his circle of advisers.

- The temple authorities did not represent the Jews. Rather than representing the Jewish people, they were, as local collaborators with imperial authority, the oppressors of the vast majority of the Jewish people. They did not represent the Jewish people any more than the collaborationist governments of Europe during World War II or during the time of the Soviet Union represented their people.

Mark's story of Jesus's trial before the temple authorities has three stages, a first one with testimony against Jesus in 14:55–59, a second one with witness by Jesus in 14:60–62, and a final one with the verdict and abuse in 14:63–65.

In the *first stage* of Jesus's trial, the witnesses disagree among themselves. Mark says twice that people "gave false testimony against him," and "their testimony did not agree" (14:56–57, 59). Mark also specifies the content of the failed accusation: "We heard him say, 'I will destroy this temple that is made with hands, and in three days I will build another, not made with hands'" (14:58). That accusation is repeated against Jesus beneath the cross: "Those who passed by derided him, shaking their heads and saying, 'Aha! You who would destroy the temple and build it in three days'" (15:29). Jesus, however, does not deign even to answer such a false accusation at his trial (14:60–61).

In the *second stage* of the trial (14:60–62), after Jesus's initial silence, because the witnesses do not agree, the high priest interrogates Jesus directly. Under Jewish law, testimony was required from "two or three" witnesses in order to convict. In the absence of witnesses who agree with each other, the high priest in effect goes for a confession, and the crucial interchange occurs. He asks, "Are you the Messiah, the Son of the Blessed One?" (14:61). That is, are you the Christ, the Son of God? That the high priest asks this question suggests that there were not "two or three witnesses" who could testify that Jesus had claimed this status for himself, which is consistent with Mark's portrayal of Jesus's message. It was not about the *person* of Jesus, but about the *kingdom of God*, which challenges the normalcy of domination systems and empires, indeed the normalcy of civilization itself.

The crucial interchange occurs with Jesus's response. Jesus says, "I am; and 'you will see the Son of Man seated at the right hand of the Power,' and 'coming with the clouds of heaven'" (14:62). His response begins with what is translated as an affirmation: "I am." But as briefly mentioned in Chapter 1, the Greek phrase *ego eimi* can be translated either as a declarative (and thus as an affirmation) or as an interrogative: "I am" or "Am I?" And, as also mentioned in Chapter 1, Matthew and Luke both read it as ambiguous. Matthew has "You have said so" (26:64); Luke has "You say that I am" (22:70). Nevertheless, the high priest apparently hears it as an affirmation, for it is the basis of his guilty verdict. It is noteworthy that Jesus is convicted on the basis of what looks like a post-Easter Christian confession of the significance of Jesus: he is the Messiah, the Son of God, who will come again.

The rest of Jesus's response shifts the topic to the "Son of Man": "'You will see the Son of Man seated at the right hand of the Power,' and 'coming with the clouds of heaven.'" Note the single quotation marks within the double quotation marks; they indicate that Jesus's response includes a quotation, specifically, language from Daniel 7 that speaks about "one like a son of man coming with the clouds of heaven" who was to be given "dominion and glory and kingship, that all peoples, nations, and languages should serve him" and whose "dominion is an everlasting dominion that shall not pass away" and whose "kingship is one that shall never be destroyed" (7:13–14). The gender-inclusive translation of "one like a son of man" (as in the New Revised Standard Version) is "one like a human being," but it is important to realize that the original language of Daniel 7:13 reads "one like a son of man," and that is the phrase that Mark echoes.

Because of the importance of Jesus's response for understanding Mark's story, we need to pause and reflect on the significance of the shift from "the Messiah, the Son of the Blessed" to "the Son of Man." Recall that, when Peter confessed Jesus as the Messiah in 8:29, Jesus did not deny it, but reinterpreted or replaced that title immediately with another one, the Son of Man destined for execution and resurrection in 8:31. Perhaps for Mark the title "Messiah" presumed a leader who would use violence to liberate

Israel from the military power of Roman imperial oppression. That was not Mark's vision of Jesus, so "Son of Man" was his preferred replacement to avoid any ambiguity between a violent and nonviolent messiah.

Mark's quotation of Daniel 7 requires careful consideration. We begin with the background of that chapter. In 167 BCE the Syrian ruler Antiochus IV Epiphanes launched a religious persecution against Jews who refused to accept full acculturation into his Hellenistic empire. Some Jews (whom we know as the Maccabees) turned to arms and fought a successful military war on earth against *his empire,* while other Jews turned to visions and the hope for an absolute divine judgment against *all empires* past, present, and future. The empires are associated with chaos, the sea, and bestial powers. The transcendental judgment of God involved a triumph of order over chaos, of sky over sea, and of the human over the bestial.

Daniel 7 records one such vision and interpretation in which God conducts a divine court case or heavenly trial against all major empires up to and including that of Antiochus IV. The Babylonian, Medean, Persian, and Macedonian empires are envisaged as beasts emerging from the chaos of the raging sea, but Alexander's Macedonians were more "terrifying and dreadful" than all that preceded them (7:4–7). His generals divided the empire among themselves and were like "horns" on that Alexander beast; Antiochus IV was the "arrogant" mini-horn (7:8, 11, 20).

In heaven "the court sat in judgment, and the books were opened" before the throne of God, the Ancient One. The decision, imagined as prophetically given *at the start* of that four-empire sequence, is for their eventual destruction. And this is to be their replacement:

As I watched in the night visions, I saw one like a human being [literally, like a son of man] coming with the clouds of

heaven. And he came to the Ancient One and was presented before him. To him was given dominion and glory
and kingship, that all peoples, nations, and languages should
serve him. His dominion is an everlasting dominion.
(7:13–14)

The fifth and final empire is given not to *one like a beast*, but to
one like a human being. The previous empires are symbolized by
beasts, the kingdom of God by a human figure. It will eventually
descend to earth and "be given to *the people* of the holy ones of
the Most High" whose "kingdom shall be an everlasting kingdom, and all dominions shall serve and obey them" (7:27). No details are given as to how, where, and when that will happen, but
God has already handed down the judgment and it is therefore
divinely inevitable.

Daniel 7 is thus an anti-imperial vision and an anti-imperial
text: the empires that have oppressed the people of God throughout the centuries are all judged negatively, and positive affirmation is given to the Son of Man, a symbol for the people of God,
to whom is given the everlasting kingdom of God. All of that is
presumed behind the extraordinary usage of the phrase "Son of
Man" for Jesus in Mark. The description "one like a son of man"
("one like a human being") from Daniel 7 has become a title, "the
Son of Man" (or "the Human One") in his version of the gospel.
It is to Jesus, then, that God's kingdom on earth has been assigned and, of course, it has been assigned to Jesus on behalf of
those designated as the people of the holy ones of God. Jesus as
Son of Man must be read against the general background of
Daniel 7 and the specific background of Mark's usage of that title
for Jesus up to that climax in 14:62. That usage has three inter-
linked aspects:

First Aspect:	Jesus as Son of Man with earthly authority	2:10, 28
Second Aspect:	Jesus as Son of Man in death and resurrection	8:31; 9:9, 12, 31; 10:33, 45; 14:21, 41
Third Aspect:	Jesus as Son of Man returning with heavenly power and glory	8:38; 13:26; 14:62

In other words, all is not future, but is rather a passage from present into future. Jesus, the Son of Man, the Human One, has already been given the kingdom of God and, even though it will be consummated in the future, it is already present on earth. That kingdom has yet to be revealed in power and glory, but it is already here in humility and service. Its presence is now known only to *faith* (1:15), but one day it will be revealed to *sight* (9:1). Mark thought that day would be "within this generation," but of course he was off on that by at least two thousand years. But, apart from that, his claim is clear. God has given the kingdom to Jesus and all are invited to enter it, *but,* as the three prophecies, reactions, and responses already made clear, that involves following Jesus through death into resurrection and a life here below absolutely opposite to the way of the world's imperial normalcy (8:34; 9:35; 10:42–45).

We return to Mark's narration of Jesus before the high priest and his council. What remains in this *third stage* of the trial is the verdict and abuse, the beginning of Jesus's physical suffering:

Then the high priest tore his clothes and said, "Why do we still need witnesses? You have heard his blasphemy! What is your decision?" All of them condemned him as deserving death. Some began to spit on him, to blindfold him, and to strike him, saying to him, "Prophesy!" The guards also took him over and beat him. (14:63–65)

Jesus has been condemned to death and he will now be handed over to Pilate. It is not yet daybreak. When day dawns on Friday, Jesus will be handed over to the Roman governor. The end—and the beginning—are near.

CONFESSION AND DENIAL

While Peter was below in the courtyard, one of the servant-girls of the high priest came by. When she saw Peter warming himself, she stared at him and said, "You also were with Jesus, the man from Nazareth." But he denied it, saying, "I do not know or understand what you are talking about." And he went out into the forecourt. Then the cock crowed. And the servant-girl, on seeing him, began again to say to the bystanders, "This man is one of them." But again he denied it. Then after a little while the bystanders again said to Peter, "Certainly you are one of them; for you are a Galilean." But he began to curse, and he swore an oath, "I do not know this man you are talking about." At that moment the cock crowed for the second time. Then Peter remembered that Jesus had said to him, "Before the cock crows twice, you will deny me three times." And he broke down and wept.

MARK 14:66–72

———— • ◆ • ————

The sequence of 14:53–72 is the last of the three *framing* units Mark created in recording the passion of Jesus. As noted at the start of Chapter 2, the denial by Peter of Jesus's ordinary identity

(Jesus of Nazareth) frames the confession by Jesus of his own extraordinary identity (Son of Man):

Incident A¹: Peter follows Jesus to the high priest's house.   14:53 – 54
Incident B: Jesus is interrogated and confesses his identity. 14:55 – 65
Incident A²: Peter is interrogated and denies Jesus.   14:66 – 72

Mark emphasizes those frames by his double mention of Peter "warming himself" in 14:54 and 14:67. And the contrast is very obvious. Peter is interrogated and responds with cowardice to unofficial bystanders. Jesus is interrogated and responds with courage to the official high priest.

Mark is, as always, writing for those Christians who had undergone lethal persecution in the Jewish homeland during the great rebellion of 66–74 CE. Mark had Jesus warn them about intrafamily betrayals and denials during those terrible years: "Brother will betray brother to death, and a father his child, and children will rise against parents and have them put to death" (13:12). The framing of Jesus's confession by Peter's denials offers those Christians a triple consolation.

First, those who imitated Jesus rather than Peter are applauded for their courage. Second, even those who imitated Peter rather than Jesus are consoled with the hope of repentance and forgiveness. Mark says that, after his denials, "Peter remembered that Jesus had said to him, 'Before the cock crows twice, you will deny me three times.' And he broke down and wept" (14:72). Third, neither denials nor even betrayals are the worst sin against Jesus or God. The worst sin is despair—loss of faith that repentance will *always, always* obtain forgiveness. Had Judas broken down, wept, and repented, he too would have been forgiven. But although Peter reappears in 16:7, Judas never reappears in Mark's story.

FRIDAY

The day of Jesus's crucifixion is the most solemn day of the Christian year. In Greek Christianity it is called "the Holy and Great Friday," in Romance languages, "Holy Friday," and in German, "Sorrowful Friday." In the English-speaking world, it is, of course "Good Friday." The origin of the English designation is uncertain; it may derive from "God's" Friday or may have begun as "Good" Friday. In either case, it may come from German, where the day was also known as *Gottes Freitag* ("God's Friday") and as *Gute Freitag* ("Good Friday").

SUBSTITUTIONARY ATONEMENT ONCE AGAIN

Though the designation of this dreadful day as "good" should strike us as incongruous, for most Christians it does not. One reason is habit, the sheer familiarity of the language. Another reason is that Christians for centuries have affirmed that on this day, despite its horror, the redemption of the world was accomplished.

The redemptive significance given to this day means that all of us who have had any exposure to Christianity have preunderstandings of what it is about. These come from centuries of Christian observance of and theological reflection about the death of Jesus.

The most familiar understanding of Jesus's death emphasizes its substitutionary sacrificial nature: he died for the sins of the world. This understanding is part of a larger package, namely, that all of us are sinners. In order for God to forgive sins, a substitutionary sacrifice must be offered. But it would not be adequate for an ordinary human being to be the sacrifice, for such a person would be a sinner and would only be dying for his or her own sins. Thus the sacrifice must not be a sinner, but a perfect human being. Only Jesus, who was not only human but also the Son of God, was perfect, spotless, and without blemish. Thus he is the sacrifice, and Good Friday is the day that makes our forgiveness possible.

For most of us who are Christian, this understanding is rooted in childhood and reinforced in our liturgies. We not only learned this as children, but our memories of Good Friday are filled with sermons on the seven last words of Jesus and hymns like "Beneath the Cross of Jesus" and "O Sacred Head Now Wounded." "Were You There When They Crucified My Lord?" elicited the confession, "Yes I was there—my sins were part of the reason Jesus had to die." Our liturgies for the Eucharist—the Mass, Communion, the Lord's Supper—commonly use the language of substitutionary sacrifice.

Thus it is not surprising that many Christians think this is the "real" reason for Jesus's death, the orthodox and "official" understanding. So do many who have difficulty with this notion, whether they remain within the church or are outside of it. The position is defended by many and viewed with skepticism, even ridiculed, by many others.

Hence it is important to realize that this is not the only Christian understanding of Jesus's death. Indeed, it took more than a thousand years for it to become dominant. The understanding sketched above first appeared in fully developed form in a book written in 1097 by St. Anselm, archbishop of Canterbury.

Anselm's argument is brilliant and, given his presuppositions, his logic is impeccable. He presupposes a legal framework for understanding our relationship with God. Our sin, our disobedience, is a crime against God. Disobedience requires punishment, or else it is not being taken seriously. Hence God must require a punishment, the payment of a price, before God can forgive our sins or crimes. Jesus is the price. The payment has been made, the debt has been satisfied. And because Jesus is provided by God, the system also affirms grace—but only within a legal framework.

This common Christian understanding goes far beyond what the New Testament says. Of course, sacrificial imagery is used there, but the language of sacrifice is only one of several different ways that the authors of the New Testament articulate the meaning of Jesus's execution. They also see it as the domination system's "no" to Jesus (and God), as the defeat of the powers that rule this world by disclosing their moral bankruptcy, as revelation of the path of transformation, and as disclosure of the depth of God's love for us.[11]

Thus, as we approach Mark's story of Friday, we need to be aware of the way in which our preunderstandings can get in the way of seeing what Mark is saying. In particular, we will argue that the substitutionary sacrificial understanding of Jesus's death is not there at all in Mark.

In addition to the tendency to see Jesus's death through the lens of later Christian doctrine, there is another problem as we seek to hear Mark's story. Namely, we most commonly hear the story of Jesus's death as a composite of the gospels and the New Testament as a whole. We do the same with the Christmas stories, the stories of Jesus's birth. From Matthew, we get the guiding star and the wise men; from Luke, we get the journey to Bethlehem, where there is no room in the inn and the shepherds are keeping watch over their flocks by night.

So also with the stories of Jesus's death. Though Matthew and Luke basically follow Mark's narrative, each differs in some respects. For example, only Matthew has the scene of Pilate washing his hands of the blood of Jesus and the cry of the crowd, "His blood be on us and on our children" (27:25), a verse that has played a significant role in Christian persecution of Jews through the centuries. Only Luke has the story of Jesus appearing before Herod Antipas as well as three of the "last words" of Jesus: "Father, forgive them; for they do not know what they are doing"; "Today you will be with me in Paradise"; and "Father, into your hands I commend my Spirit" (23:34, 43, 46).

The story of Good Friday in John's gospel contains much more dialogue between Jesus and Pilate (in Mark, Jesus speaks to Pilate only once and then is silent). John also adds three more "last words" from the cross: to his mother and the beloved disciple, "Woman, here is your son" and "Here is your mother"; "I am thirsty"; and "It is finished" (19:26–28, 30). Finally, the composite understanding of Good Friday commonly includes language from Paul and the author of the letter to the Hebrews: Jesus as the sacrifice for sin and as the great high priest who offers himself as the sacrifice (9: 11–14).

Thus it requires significant effort to hear how Mark tells the story without the filters provided by other books of the New Testament and later Christian theology. These filters are not simply wrong or to be dismissed. But we need to set them aside if we are to hear Mark's story as he tells it.

MARK'S STORY OF GOOD FRIDAY

As the earliest gospel, Mark provides the earliest narrative of the crucifixion. Of course, he is not the first to mention it. That honor belongs to Paul, all of whose genuine letters were written before any of the gospels. Paul refers to the fact of Jesus's crucifixion many times: he speaks again and again of Jesus's death, of the cross and Christ crucified. It is "the wisdom and power of God," though it is "a stumbling block" to Jews and "foolishness" to Gentiles. It is the demonstration of God's love for us, the sacrifice that makes our redemption possible, and the path of personal transformation as dying and rising that lies at the heart of the Christian life (1 Cor. 1:23–24; Rom. 5:8; 3:24–25; Gal. 2:19–20; Rom. 6:3–4).[12]

Occasionally he says a bit more about what happened. In one passage, he refers to both Jesus's death and burial: "Christ died for our sins in accordance with the scriptures, and he was buried." In another, he tells us that "the rulers of this age . . . crucified the Lord of glory." In a letter attributed to him, he or a follower says that in the cross, God "disarmed the rulers and authorities and made a public example of them, triumphing over them in it" (1 Cor. 15:3–4; 2:8; Col. 2:15).

But Paul's letters are not narratives and thus do not include a story of Good Friday. Instead, as the examples of his language above indicate, his letters contain a number of interpretations of the significance of Jesus's death. That Paul, the earliest author in the New Testament, uses multiple interpretations leads to an important point: there is no uninterpreted account of the death of Jesus in the New Testament. It is not difficult to see why. The followers of Jesus in the years and decades after his death sought to see meaning in the horrific execution of their beloved master, whom they saw as God's anointed one. Looking back upon this event, they retrospectively see providential purpose in it.

So also in Mark's gospel. Though Mark provides the earliest story of Good Friday, we should not imagine that his story is thus free of post-Easter interpretation. Mark's narrative combines retrospective interpretation with history remembered.

Mark tells the story of Good Friday in precisely indicated three-hour intervals: from dawn (6 AM) to 9 AM, from 9 AM to noon, from noon to 3 PM, and from 3 PM to evening (6 PM). We will first review his story as a combination of history and interpretation and then explore his larger interpretive framework.

From 6 to 9 AM

As soon as it was morning, the chief priests held a consultation with the elders and scribes and the whole council. They bound Jesus, led him away, and handed him over to Pilate. Pilate asked him, "Are you the King of the Jews?" He answered him, "You say so." Then the chief priests accused him of many things. Pilate asked him again, "Have you no answer? See how many charges they bring against you." But Jesus made no further reply, so that Pilate was amazed.

Now at the festival he used to release a prisoner for them, anyone for whom they asked. Now a man called Barabbas was in prison with the rebels who had committed murder during the insurrection. So the crowd came and began to ask Pilate to do for them according to his custom. Then he answered them, "Do you want me to release for you the King of the Jews?" For he realized that it was out of jealousy that the chief priests had handed him over. But the chief priests stirred up the crowd to have him release Barabbas for them instead. Pilate spoke to them again, "Then what do you wish me to do with the man you call the King of the Jews?" They shouted back, "Crucify him!" Pilate asked them, "Why, what evil has he done?" But they shouted all the more, "Crucify him!" So Pilate, wishing to satisfy the crowd, released Barabbas for them; and after flogging Jesus, he handed him over to be crucified.

Then the soldiers led him into the courtyard of the palace (that is, the governor's headquarters); and they called together the whole cohort. And they clothed him in a purple cloak; and after twisting some thorns into a crown, they put it on him. And they began saluting him, "Hail, King of the Jews!" They struck his head with a reed, spat upon him, and knelt down in homage to him. After mocking him, they stripped him of the purple cloak and put his own clothes on him. Then they led him out to crucify him.

They compelled a passer-by, who was coming in from the country, to carry his cross; it was Simon of Cyrene, the father of Alexander and Rufus.

MARK 15:1–21

As day breaks, the local collaborators—chief priests, elders, and scribes—hand over Jesus to Pilate, the local representative of imperial authority. Pilate interrogates Jesus. Mark does not tell us where this happens, but almost certainly it occurs in the palace of the late king Herod the Great, where the Roman governors normally stayed while they were in Jerusalem. Later, Mark refers explicitly to "the courtyard of the palace" (15:16). As the scene unfolds, it is clear that the local authorities are also present.

Pilate asks Jesus, "Are you the King of the Jews?" We should probably hear a mocking emphasis on the word "you" in Pilate's question. "*You*"—a Jewish peasant, already beaten, bloodied, and bound, standing powerless before me—"are the king of the Jews?" So also we should probably hear in Jesus's response a mocking emphasis on the same word: "*You* say so."[13]

Hearing this as nonresponsive, Pilate presses his question: "Have you no answer? See how many charges they bring against you." But, Mark tells us, "Jesus made no further reply" (15:5). To refuse to respond to authority reflects both courage and contempt. Authorities do not like it. Pilate is amazed. Indeed, Jesus does not speak again in Mark's story until his final cry from the cross later in the day: "My God, my God, why have you forsaken me?" (15:34).

Then follows the puzzling episode of Pilate offering to release any prisoner the crowd wished, puzzling because it is difficult to imagine that such a practice existed in a troublesome province like Judea. As Mark tells the story, it involves a rebel named

Barabbas, who had committed murder during the "insurrection."
Pilate asks, "Do you want me to release for you the King of the
Jews [that is, Jesus]?" But, Mark tells us, the temple authorities
"stirred up the crowd to have him release Barabbas for them instead" (15:11).

Almost certainly, this is not the same crowd that heard Jesus
with delight during the week; Mark gives us no reason to think
that crowd has turned against Jesus. Moreover, it is highly unlikely that the crowd from earlier in the week would be allowed
into Herod's palace, where this scene is set. *This* crowd, the
crowd stirred up by the chief priests, must have been much
smaller and is best understood as provided by the authorities
(somebody had to let them into the palace). When Pilate asks
this crowd, "Then what do you wish me to do with the man you
call the King of the Jews?" they respond, "Crucify him" (15:13).
So Pilate releases Barabbas and hands Jesus over to his soldiers
to be crucified.

As history remembered, the story about Barabbas is difficult.
But if we set it in Mark's historical context as he wrote around
the year 70, it makes considerable sense. Both Barabbas and Jesus
are revolutionaries. Both defied imperial authority. But the first
advocated violent revolution and the second advocated nonviolence. By the year 66, the Jerusalem crowd (and many others in
the Jewish homeland) had chosen the way of Barabbas, not the
way of Jesus. The events of 66–70 make this story intelligible.

The first three hours of the day continue to unfold. Having
been handed over to Pilate's soldiers, Jesus, like so many political
prisoners before and after him, is tortured and humiliated. He is
flogged. Then the soldiers undress him (itself an indication of
his powerlessness in their hands) and put him through a mock
coronation ceremony: they clothe him with a purple cloak, put a
crown (of thorns) on his head, hail him as "King of the Jews,"
strike him, and spit on him. Then they undress him again, put his
own clothes back on him, and lead him out to be crucified.

Prisoners condemned to death by crucifixion were normally required to carry the horizontal bar of the cross to the place of execution, where the vertical bar was a post permanently positioned
in the ground. But Mark tells us that the soldiers compelled a
passerby, Simon of Cyrene, to carry Jesus's cross. Though Mark
does not say why, presumably it was not an act of kindness toward
Jesus, but because Jesus had become too weak to carry the
wooden beam himself.

From 9 AM to Noon

Then they brought Jesus to the place called Golgotha
(which means the place of a skull). And they offered him
wine mixed with myrrh; but he did not take it. And they
crucified him, and divided his clothes among them, casting
lots to decide what each should take.

It was nine o'clock in the morning when they crucified
him. The inscription of the charge against him read, "The
King of the Jews." And with him they crucified two bandits,
one on his right and one on his left. Those who passed by
derided him, shaking their heads and saying, "Aha! You who
would destroy the temple and build it in three days, save
yourself, and come down from the cross!" In the same way
the chief priests, along with the scribes, were also mocking
him among themselves and saying, "He saved others; he
cannot save himself. Let the Messiah, the King of Israel,
come down from the cross now, so that we may see and believe." Those who were crucified with him also taunted him.

MARK 15:22–32

At 9 AM, at a place named Golgotha, "the place of a skull," the
soldiers crucify Jesus. Mark refers to the event itself with only a
short phrase: "And they crucified him" (15:24). He did not need to

say more, for his community was very familiar with the Roman practice of crucifixion. But we today may need some explanation.

Crucifixion was a form of Roman imperial terrorism. First and above all else, although the Romans did not invent it, they reserved it for very special victims. Next, it was not just capital punishment, but a very definite type of capital punishment for those such as runaway slaves or rebel insurgents who subverted Roman law and order and thereby disturbed the Pax Romana (the "Roman peace"). Furthermore, as imperial terrorism, it was always as public as possible—it was a calculated social deterrent and as such it had to very, very public. Its victims were hung up as a public warning. Finally, along with other supreme penalties, such as being burned alive or eaten alive by beasts, what made it *supreme* was not just the amount of suffering or even humiliation involved, but that there might be nothing left or allowed for burial.

As a form of public terrorism, the uprights of the crosses were usually permanently in place just outside a city gate on a high or prominent place. The victim usually carried or dragged the crossbar along with notice of the crime to be attached to one of those uprights at the place of execution. The only crucified body ever discovered in the Jewish homeland was a first-century victim whose arms were roped over the crossbar and whose ankle bones were pierced by iron nails on either side of the upright. Although he was given an honorable burial in his family tomb, other victims were often crucified low enough to the ground that not only carrion birds but scavenging dogs could reach them. And they were often left on the cross after death until little was left of their bodies even for a possible burial.

At the site of crucifixion the soldiers cast lots for Jesus's garments, a point to which we will return when we describe Mark's larger interpretive framework. As Jesus hangs on the cross, he is mocked, presumably by the same people who had accused him before the high priest, for they repeat the accusation: "You who

would destroy the temple and build it in three days, save yourself
and come down from the cross!" (15:29, echoing 14:58). Among
themselves, the chief priests and scribes also mocked him: "Let
the Messiah, the King of Israel, come down from the cross!"

On the cross was an inscription: "The King of the Jews." From
Mark's point of view, the inscription is ironic. Pilate intended it as
derision and most likely saw it as mocking not only Jesus, but his
accusers, as if to say, "This person whom Rome has the power to
execute is your king—some king." Yet from the vantage point of
Mark and early Christianity, the inscription, despite its derisory
intention, is accurate. Jesus is the true king.

Mark tells us that Jesus was crucified between two "bandits."
The Greek word translated "bandits" is commonly used for
guerilla fighters against Rome, who were either "terrorists" or
"freedom fighters," depending upon one's point of view. Their
presence in the story reminds us that crucifixion was used specifically for people who systematically refused to accept Roman imperial authority. Ordinary criminals were not crucified. Jesus is
executed as a rebel against Rome between two other rebels
against Rome.

The common impression that they were "robbers" rather than
insurrectionists is based upon Luke's story of the dialogue between Jesus and "the repentant thief," which ends with Jesus saying, "Today you will be with me in Paradise" (23:39–43). But in
Mark there is no such dialogue. Indeed, we are told that "those
who were crucified with him also taunted him" (15:32)

From Noon to 3 PM

When it was noon, darkness came over the whole land until
three in the afternoon.

MARK 15:33

——•◆•——

Jesus has now been on the cross for three hours. The next three hours, from noon until 3 PM, are described with a single sentence: "When it was noon, darkness came over the land until three in the afternoon." The Greek word translated "land" can also mean "earth," and it is unclear whether Mark means the land (presumably Judea) or the earth as a whole.

Interpreters have occasionally suggested that the cause of the darkness may have been an eclipse of the sun, but this explanation is impossible. Even during a total eclipse of the sun, darkness lasts for only a few minutes, not hours. Moreover, because astronomers can tell us when and where total eclipses have occurred, we know there was not one in this part of the world anytime near the year 30. That it was a "supernatural" darkness is also exceedingly unlikely. Not only would this require an interventionist understanding of God's relation to nature, but an inexplicable darkness of this duration most likely would have been remarked upon by non-Christian authors, and we have no such reports.

Instead, the darkness is the product of Mark's use of religious symbolism. In the ancient world, highly significant events on earth were accompanied by signs in the sky. A comet signified the death of Julius Caesar. So also with darkness: across cultures, darkness is an archetypal image associated with suffering, mourning, and judgment. Such usage appears in Mark's sacred scripture, the Jewish Bible. In the exodus story, one of the plagues involved "darkness over the land" (Exod. 10:21–23). In the prophets, darkness is associated with mourning and God's judgment. In a reproach to Jerusalem from the sixth century BCE, Jeremiah refers to the sun setting at midday (15:9). In texts of judgment, Zephaniah and Joel refer to a day of "darkness and gloom" (Zeph. 1:15; Joel 2:2, 31). In a passage that threatens judgment upon Israel in the eighth century BCE, Amos says in the name of God, "I will make the sun go down at noon and darken the earth in broad daylight" (8:9).

Given this background, the darkness from noon to 3 PM is best understood as literary symbolism. How many resonances of meaning Mark intended is unclear, but it is reasonable to imagine a combination of grief and judgment. The cosmos itself joins in mourning what is happening, even as the darkness symbolizes judgment upon the rulers responsible for crucifying "the Lord of glory," to use language from Paul.

From 3 to 6 PM

At three o'clock Jesus cried out with a loud voice, "Eloi, Eloi, lema sabachthani?" which means, "My God, my God, why have you forsaken me?" When some of the bystanders heard it, they said, "Listen, he is calling for Elijah." And someone ran, filled a sponge with sour wine, put it on a stick, and gave it to him to drink, saying, "Wait, let us see whether Elijah will come to take him down." Then Jesus gave a loud cry and breathed his last. And the curtain of the temple was torn in two, from top to bottom. Now when the centurion, who stood facing him, saw that in this way he breathed his last, he said, "Truly this man was God's Son!"

There were also women looking on from a distance; among them were Mary Magdalene, and Mary the mother of James the younger and of Joses, and Salome. These used to follow him and provided for him when he was in Galilee; and there were many other women who had come up with him to Jerusalem.

MARK 15:34−41

At 3 PM or shortly thereafter, Jesus "gave a loud cry and breathed his last." Mark reports his last and only words from the cross as, "My God, my God, why have you forsaken me?" A scream of desolation, it is a quotation from Psalm 22. We will return to this when we describe Mark's larger interpretive framework.

Then Mark narrates two events that provide two interpretive comments about what has happened. The first is the tearing of the temple curtain: "And the curtain of the temple was torn in two, from top to bottom" (15:38). As with the darkness from noon to 3 PM , this event is best understood symbolically and not as history remembered.

The curtain separated the holiest part of the temple sanctuary—the Holy of Holies—from the rest of the sanctuary. The Holy of Holies was understood to be the particular place of God's presence: God was most present, concentratedly present, in the innermost part of the sanctuary. So sacred was this part of the sanctuary that only the high priest was permitted to enter it, and only on one day of the year.

To say, as Mark does, that the curtain was torn in two has a twofold meaning. On the one hand, it is a judgment upon the temple and the temple authorities, the local authorities who colluded with imperial Rome to condemn Jesus to death. On the other hand, it is an affirmation. To say that the curtain, the veil, has been torn is to affirm that the execution of Jesus means that access to the presence of God is now open. This affirmation underlines Mark's presentation of Jesus earlier in the gospel: Jesus mediated access to God apart from the temple and the domination system that it had come to represent in the first century.

Then Mark narrates a second event contemporaneous with Jesus's death. The imperial centurion in command of the soldiers who had crucified Jesus exclaims, "Truly this man was God's Son" (15:30). He is the first human in Mark's gospel to call Jesus "God's Son." Not even Jesus's followers speak of him this way in Mark's story.

That this exclamation comes from a centurion is very significant. According to Roman imperial theology, the emperor was "Son of God"—the revelation of God's power and will for the earth. According to the same theology, the emperor was Lord, Savior, and the one who had brought peace on earth. But now a representative of Rome affirms that this man, Jesus, executed by the empire, is the Son of God. Thus the emperor is not. In the exclamation of the centurion responsible for Jesus's execution, who saw him up close, empire testifies against itself.

There are more witnesses to Jesus's death. From afar, but close enough to see, his women followers watch:

> There were also women looking on from a distance. Among them were Mary Magdalene, and Mary the mother of James the younger and of Joses, and Salome. These used to follow him and provided for him when he was in Galilee; and there were many other women who had come up with him to Jerusalem. (15:40–41)

From what is said about Mary Magdalene in other gospels, she was the most important of Jesus's women followers. About the other Mary, "the mother of James the younger and of Joses," we know nothing. About the third woman, we can say only that Salome was a common woman's name in the first century.

The presence of the women reminds us that Jesus's men followers are not present. They have all fled. Perhaps it was safer for women to be nearby; they were less likely to be suspected by the authorities of being dangerous subversives.

Whatever the reason, in Mark (and all the gospels) women play a major role in the story of Good Friday and Easter. They witness Jesus's death. They follow his body after his death and see where he is buried. In all the gospels, they are the first ones to go to the tomb on Sunday and experience the news of Easter. In Mark, as we shall see in our chapter on Easter Sunday, they are the only ones.

The role of women in Mark's story of Good Friday raises an interesting question. Why would first-century Jewish women (and slightly later, gentile women) be attracted to Jesus? For the same reasons that first-century men were, yes. But in addition it seems clear that Jesus and earliest Christianity gave to women an identity and status that they did not experience within the conventional wisdom of the time. Women in both Jewish and gentile cultures were subordinated in many ways. Jesus and the early Christian movement subverted the conventional wisdom about women among both Jews and gentiles. The subversion has been denied by much of Christian history, but it is right here, in a prominent place in the story of the climactic events of Jesus's life: Good Friday and Easter.

6 PM and the Burial of Jesus

When evening had come, and since it was the day of Preparation, that is, the day before the sabbath, Joseph of Arimathea, a respected member of the council, who was also himself waiting expectantly for the kingdom of God, went boldly to Pilate and asked for the body of Jesus. Then Pilate wondered if he were already dead; and summoning the centurion, he asked him whether he had been dead for some time. When he learned from the centurion that he was dead, he granted the body to Joseph. Then Joseph bought a linen cloth, and taking down the body, wrapped it in the linen cloth, and laid it in a tomb that had been hewn out of the rock. He then rolled a stone against the door of the tomb. Mary Magdalene and Mary the mother of Jesus saw where the body was laid.

MARK 15:42–47

It has been a long day. Now evening approaches, around 6 PM in the Jewish homeland in the spring of the year. Sunset will mark the beginning of sabbath.

Apparently anxious that Jesus's body be removed from the cross and buried before the sabbath began, Joseph of Arimathea, described by Mark as "a respected member of the council who was also himself waiting expectantly for the kingdom of God," asks Pilate for permission to do so. After receiving verification that Jesus had been dead for some time, Pilate grants his request. Joseph then arranges for the body to be taken down, wrapped in a linen cloth, placed in a tomb hewn out of rock, and then sealed in the tomb by a stone rolled across its door. This is a remarkable departure from customary procedure since, as mentioned earlier, the body of a crucified individual was not given an honorable burial.

The story of Jesus's burial by Joseph grows in the other gospels. In Mark, Joseph is not described as a follower of Jesus, but at most might be viewed as a sympathizer. Matthew calls him "a disciple of Jesus" (27:57). Luke does not call Joseph a disciple, but adds that he was "a good and righteous man who had not agreed" with the council's condemnation of Jesus (23:50–51). To Mark's account, Matthew adds that it was Joseph's own tomb and new (27:60). Though Luke does not say it was Joseph's tomb, he does say that it was new: no one had ever yet been laid in it (23:53). John also says that the tomb was new, and that Nicodemus (mentioned only in John) assisted Joseph and brought a hundred pounds of myrrh and aloes, an enormous amount of spices (19:38–42). In John, Jesus is in effect given a royal burial.

Whatever the history behind the story of Jesus's burial, in Mark it sets the stage for Easter morning. Jesus's women disciples, having followed Joseph, see where his body has been entombed.

JESUS'S DEATH AS SACRIFICE?

We return to a common Christian understanding of Jesus's death: that it was a substitutionary sacrifice for the sins of the world. As we reflect on the extent to which this is present in Mark, we distinguish between a broad and a more specific meaning of the word "sacrifice."

The broad meaning refers to sacrificing one's life for a cause. It is common to refer to Martin Luther King, Jr., Mohandas Gandhi, Oscar Romero, and Dietrich Bonhoeffer as sacrificing their lives for the causes to which they were devoted. Soldiers killed in action are often described as sacrificing their lives for their country. In this sense, one may speak of Jesus sacrificing his life for his passion, namely, for his advocacy of the kingdom of God.

The more specific meaning of sacrifice in relation to Jesus's death speaks of it as a substitutionary sacrifice *for sin*, a dying for the sins of the world. This understanding is absent from Mark's story of Good Friday; it is not there at all.

Indeed, this understanding may be absent from Mark's gospel as a whole. The three anticipations of Jesus's death in the central section of Mark do not say that Jesus must go to Jerusalem in order to die for the sins of the world. Rather, they refer to Jerusalem as the place of execution by the authorities. There is only one passage in all of Mark that might have a substitutionary sacrificial meaning. It is the passage in which, after the third anticipation of his death, as the Jesus of Mark speaks to his followers a third time about what it means to follow him, he says: "The Son of Man came not to be served but to serve, and to give his life a *ransom* for many" (10:45).

To many Christians, the word "ransom" sounds like sacrificial language, for we sometimes speak of Jesus as the ransom for our sins. But it almost certainly does not have this meaning in Mark. As already mentioned, the Greek word translated as "ransom" (*lutron*) is used in the Bible not in the context of payment for sin, but to refer to payment made to liberate captives (often from captivity in war) or slaves (often from debt slavery). A *lutron* is a means of liberation from bondage.

Thus to say that Jesus gave "his life a *ransom* for many" means he gave his life as a means of liberation from bondage. The context of the passage in Mark supports this reading. The preceding verses are a critique of the domination system: the rulers of the nations lord it over their subjects, and their great ones are tyrants (10:42). "It is not so among you," Jesus says, and then uses his own path as an illustration. In contrast to the rulers of this world, "The Son of Man came not to be served but to serve, and to give his life a *lutron*—a means of liberation—for many." And this is a path for his followers to imitate: so it shall be "among you."

Thus Mark does not understand the death of Jesus as a substitutionary sacrifice for sin. Claims to the contrary can only point to a mistaken reading of the single passage we have just explored.

How then does Mark understand Jesus's death? As his story of Good Friday reports, he sees Jesus's death as an execution by the authorities because of his challenge to the domination system. The decision of the temple authorities to take action against him was made after his disruptive act in the temple. These local collaborators handed him over to imperial authority, which then crucified him on a charge that was simultaneously and indissolubly political and religious: "King of the Jews."

As such, Mark understands Jesus's death as a judgment on the authorities and the temple. The "chief priests, elders, and scribes" have killed him, just as Jesus said they would. Judgment is indicated by the fact that, as Jesus dies, darkness comes over the city and land, and the great curtain in the temple is torn in two. And a Roman centurion pronounces judgment against his own empire, which has just killed Jesus: "Truly this man—and not the emperor—is God's Son."

MARK'S USE OF THE JEWISH BIBLE

At several points in his story of Good Friday, Mark echoes and sometimes quotes the Jewish Bible. Before describing how this shapes his interpretive framework, we will comment about a common Christian way of seeing the relationship between what we call the Old Testament and the New Testament.

Many of us who grew up Christian were taught that the relationship between the two testaments is one of prophecy and fulfillment. The Old Testament prophesies the coming of the Messiah, and this is fulfilled in Jesus. This relationship of prophecy and fulfillment was commonly understood as *prediction* and fulfillment. Many of us learned that there were scores of predictions of Jesus and the events of his life in the Old Testament. These not only demonstrated that Jesus was the Messiah, but also proved the truth of the Bible and thus Christianity—only a supernaturally inspired scripture could predict the future so precisely.

This way of seeing the relationship between the two testaments has an important effect upon how the life and death of Jesus are seen. It easily and naturally, if not inevitably, leads to the inference that things had to happen this way. These events were foreknown, foreordained, are part of God's "plan of salvation." They happened through divine destiny and even necessity. Divine destiny: God planned it this way. Divine necessity: it had to happen this way. And this often connects to the substitutionary sacrificial understanding of Jesus's death as well: Jesus's death was foreordained and necessary because God can forgive sins only through adequate substitutionary sacrifice.

We see the relationship between the Jewish Bible and the New Testament very differently, as mainstream scholarship in general does. The Jewish Bible was the sacred scripture of early Christians, and many of them knew it well, whether from hearing it orally or being able to read it. Thus, as they told the story of Jesus, they used language from the Jewish Bible to do so.

This practice produced what we call "prophecy historicized." A passage from the past (in this case, from the Jewish Bible) is "historicized" when it is used in the narration of a subsequent story (the gospels and the New Testament). "Historicizing" here does not make something historical or historically factual. It simply means using an older passage in a newer story in an attempt to connect that newer story to the earlier tradition and lend credibility to it.

To illustrate the process, we use two examples from Matthew, the master of prophecy historicized. In his story of Jesus's infancy, Jesus and his family return from Egypt after their flight there to escape the persecution of Herod. Matthew says their return fulfills a passage from the prophet Hosea: "Out of Egypt have I called my son" (11:1). In Hosea this passage refers to the exodus. It speaks of God's love for Israel and the things God has done for it, especially deliverance during the exodus—God's "calling his son," Israel, "out of Egypt." Matthew takes that passage and says that it refers to God's calling his "son"—Jesus—out of Egypt. This is prophecy historicized: using a passage from the Old Testament in the telling of a subsequent story.

In a second example, as Matthew tells the story of Judas's suicide near the end of his gospel, he historicizes a passage from the prophets by connecting it to the price of Jesus's betrayal, thirty pieces of silver. In 27:9, Matthew echoes a passage from Zechariah 11:13 (wrongly attributing it to Jeremiah), that refers to thirty shekels of silver being returned to the temple treasury.

It is sometimes difficult to discern whether "prophecy historicized" is being used to comment about something that actually happened or whether it is being used to generate a narrative or a detail within a narrative. But such discernment is not our present concern. The point, rather, is the use of passages from the Jewish Bible in the telling of the story of Jesus and *what such use suggests about the interpretive framework of the narrator.*

With this prologue complete, we now turn to Mark's use of the Jewish Bible in the story of Good Friday. We have seen some of this already, for example, in the use of the darkness at midday motif. Now we focus on his primary use of the Jewish Bible, namely, his frequent citation of Psalm 22. Its opening words are the final words of Jesus: "My God, my God, why have you forsaken me?" The story of the soldiers casting lots for the clothes of Jesus echoes Psalm 22:18: "They divide my clothes among themselves, and for my clothing they cast lots." Two phrases from Psalm 22:7 are echoed when Mark says Jesus is "mocked" by people "shaking their heads" (15:29, 31).

How are these references to be understood? Within the common Christian framework of prediction and fulfillment, the psalm is understood as if it contained predictions of details of Jesus's death. Within the framework of "prophecy historicized," they are seen as the product of Mark's use of the psalm as a way of interpreting the death of Jesus. Whether the psalm is generating some of the details of the story or whether it is being used to comment on things that did happen is, as often, difficult to know. For example, did Jesus really quote the opening verse as he died? It is possible. And did soldiers really gamble for a peasant's clothes, or did the psalm generate this detail? Either seems possible. But the point, once again, is what the use of Psalm 22 suggests about Mark's interpretive framework.

As part of the Jewish Bible, Psalm 22 is a prayer for deliverance. The prayer describes a person experiencing immense suffering and intense hostility. Like Job, the sufferer does not understand why he is suffering, but feels forsaken by God, to whom he has been faithful. Though he has trusted in God from birth, now in his extremity he is scorned, despised, and mocked. He feels abandoned by everybody, friends and God. He fears he is near death:

> I am poured out like water, and all my bones are out of joint; my heart is like wax; it is melted within my breast; my mouth is dried up like a potsherd, and my tongue sticks to my jaws; you lay me in the dust of death. . . . I can count all my bones. (22:14–17)

Indeed, he feels so close to death that the onlookers are beginning to divide up his possessions: "They stare and gloat over me; they divide my clothes among themselves, and for my clothing they cast lots." Such seems to be the meaning of this passage in the context of the psalm itself.

Then the mood of the psalm changes. The desperate suffering and anguished abandonment of the first half becomes in the second half a prayer of thanksgiving for deliverance and vindication. The two parts combine to create a psalm of pain and deliverance, of a righteous sufferer crying out and then being vindicated by God.

Mark's frequent use of language from this psalm suggests that he and his community saw the death of Jesus this way. It was the suffering and death of one who was righteous, condemned by the powers of this world, and who would be vindicated by God.

Our point is not that Mark saw Jesus's cry of abandonment as really pointing toward vindication, as is occasionally suggested by interpreters who find it difficult to imagine that Jesus could really have felt forsaken by God. Mark saw the anguish as real. Our point, rather, is that Mark's use of this psalm suggests the larger framework within which he understood Jesus's death as a whole. It would lead to vindication. For Mark, as for other early Christians, the story of Good Friday is incomplete without Easter.

DIVINE NECESSITY OR HUMAN INEVITABILITY?

Did Jesus's death have to happen? There are two quite different reasons why one might think so. One is divine necessity; the other is human inevitability. We begin with the first. Did it have to happen because it was the will of God? We have already touched upon this subject when we described the effects of seeing passages in the Jewish Bible as "predictions" of the life and death of Jesus. Now we raise it for an additional reason. This question has something to teach us as we reflect about the meaning and significance of Good Friday.

As mentioned earlier in this chapter, by the time Mark wrote, early Christianity had already developed several interpretations of the death of Jesus. All are purposive and providential: through this event, God has accomplished something of great value. And all are retrospective and retrojective: they look back on the death of Jesus and see providential purpose in it that had not occurred to his followers before or immediately at the time of his death, and they retroject this purpose back into the story.

This easily generates the inference that Jesus's death had to happen. But is this inference either correct or necessary? We begin our reflection about this question with a story from the Jewish Bible in which we see the same combination of retrospection and retrojection. Found in Genesis 37–50, it is a story about Joseph and his brothers, the fathers of the twelve tribes of Israel. Out of envy, his brothers sell Joseph into slavery when he is young and he ends up in Egypt. Over the decades he rises to a position of authority second only to Pharaoh, the ruler of Egypt. Famine strikes the land of Canaan, and Joseph's brothers come to Egypt seeking food. They do not know what has happened to Joseph, or even if he is still alive.

Then Joseph meets with them and, understandably, they are afraid. Their brother whom they sold into slavery out of sheer malice now has the power of life and death over them. As second in power to Pharaoh, he can do with them whatever he wants. But Joseph is not vengeful. Instead he says:

> Do not be distressed or angry with yourselves because you sold me here; *for God sent me* before you to preserve life.... *God sent me* before you to preserve for you a remnant on earth, and to keep alive for you many survivors. So it was not you who sent me here, *but God.* (Gen. 45:5–7)

As the author of Genesis tells the story, Joseph affirms a providential purpose in his being sold into slavery: "*God sent me*—it was not you who sent me here, *but God.*"

Does Joseph's affirmation—"God sent me"—mean that it was the will of God that his brothers sell him into slavery? No—for it is never the will of God to sell your brother into slavery. Did it have to happen this way? No—it could have happened differently; one can imagine the brothers not selling Joseph into slavery. Presumably they were not foreordained to decide to do so. The retrospective retrojection of purpose into the story does not require that we think of it as God's will or that it had to happen this way. Rather, the story affirms that even the evil deed of selling a brother into slavery was used by God for a providential purpose.

Applying this story of Joseph, how might we see the story of Good Friday? Was the death of Jesus the will of God? No. It is never the will of God that a righteous man be crucified. Did it have to happen? It might have turned out differently. Judas might not have betrayed Jesus. The temple authorities might have decided on a course of action other than recommending execution. Pilate might have let Jesus go or decided on a punishment other than death. But it did happen this way. And like the storyteller of Genesis, early Christian storytellers looking back on what did happen ascribe providential meanings to Good Friday. But this does not mean Good Friday had to happen.

But for another reason the execution of Jesus was virtually inevitable. Not because of divine necessity, but because of human inevitability—this is what domination systems did to people who publicly and vigorously challenged them. It happened often in the ancient world. It has happened to countless people throughout history. Closer to Jesus, it had happened to his mentor John the Baptizer, arrested and executed by Herod Antipas not long before. Now it happened to Jesus. Within a few more decades, it would happen to Paul, Peter, and James. We should wonder what it was about Jesus and his movement that so provoked the authorities at the top of the domination systems of their time.

But Jesus was not simply an unfortunate victim of a domination system's brutality. He was also a protagonist filled with passion. His passion, his message, was about the kingdom of God.

He spoke to peasants as a voice of peasant religious protest against the central economic and political institutions of his day. He attracted a following and took his movement to Jerusalem at the season of Passover. There he challenged the authorities with public acts and public debates. All of this was his passion, what he was passionate about: God and the kingdom of God, God and God's passion for justice.

Jesus's passion got him killed. To put this meaning of passion and a narrower meaning of passion into a single sentence: Jesus's passion for the kingdom of God led to what is often called his passion, namely, his suffering and death. But to restrict Jesus's passion to his suffering and death is to ignore the passion that brought him to Jerusalem. To think of Jesus's passion as simply what happened on Good Friday is to separate his death from the passion that animated his life.

Now to return to the question with which this section began. Did Good Friday have to happen? As divine necessity? No. As human inevitability? Virtually. Good Friday is the result of the collision between the passion of Jesus and the domination systems of his time.

It is important to realize that what killed Jesus was nothing unusual. We have no reason to think that the temple authorities were wicked people. Moreover, as empires go, Rome was better than most. There was nothing exceptional or abnormal about it; this is simply the way domination systems behave. So common is this dynamic that, as we suggested early in this book, it can also be called the normalcy of civilization. At a broad level of generalization, Good Friday was the result of the collision between the passion of Jesus and the normalcy of civilization.

This realization generates an additional reflection. According to Mark, Jesus did not die *for* the sins of the world. The language of substitutionary sacrifice for sin is absent from his story. But in an important sense, he was killed *because* of the sin of the world. It was the injustice of domination systems that killed him, injustice so routine that it is part of the normalcy of civilization. Though sin means more than this, it includes this. And thus Jesus was crucified because of the sin of the world.

We conclude this chapter with one more question. Was Jesus guilty or innocent? Because language familiar to Christians speaks of Jesus as sinless, perfect, righteous, spotless, and without blemish, the question will seem surprising to some. But it is worth reflecting about.

As Mark tells the story, Jesus was not only executed by the method used to execute violent insurrectionists; he was physically executed between two insurrectionists. Was Jesus guilty of advocating violent revolution against the empire and its local collaborators? No.

As Mark tells the story, was Jesus guilty of claiming to be the Messiah, the Son of the Blessed? Perhaps. Why perhaps and not a simple yes? Mark does not report that Jesus taught this, and his account of Jesus's response to the high priest's question about this is at least a bit ambiguous.

As Mark tells the story, was Jesus guilty of nonviolent resistance to imperial Roman oppression and local Jewish collaboration? Oh, yes. Mark's story of Jesus's final week is a sequence of public demonstrations against and confrontations with the domination system. And, as all know, it killed him.

——— · ◆ · ———

SEVEN

SATURDAY

A fter detailing every day from Sunday through Friday of Holy
Week, Mark says nothing at all about the sabbath. After detailing the hours of Friday in three-hour intervals corresponding
to the legionary watch periods, Mark says nothing about Saturday. He notes that Jesus was crucified and buried on "the day of
Preparation, that is, the day before the sabbath" (15:42). Then he
picks up the story on Easter Sunday with the finding of the
empty tomb: "When the sabbath was over, Mary Magdalene, and
Mary the mother of James, and Salome bought spices, so that
they might go and anoint him" (16:1). But what about that sabbath itself? What about the day we call Holy Saturday? Was there
nothing to say about that day in earliest Christian tradition, or
has Mark omitted what others have recorded? And, if we Christians have followed Mark's silence about Holy Saturday, have we
lost something in the process?

You can see very clearly what Mark has omitted by comparing
the two most familiar creeds of the church, the Apostles' Creed
and the Nicene Creed, as they detail the last days of Holy Week.
The Apostles' Creed has three events on three separate days:

Friday:	Suffered under Pontius Pilate;
	was crucified, dead, and buried.
Saturday:	He descended into hell.
Sunday:	The third day he rose again from the dead.

But the Nicene Creed has only two events on two separate days and what is missing, as in Mark, is anything about Jesus and Holy Saturday:

Friday: For our sake he was crucified under Pontius Pilate;
               he suffered death and was buried.
Sunday: On the third day he rose again in accordance
               with the Scriptures.

The event—"he descended into hell"—mentioned in the Apostles' Creed but omitted in the Nicene Creed is known as the "descent into hell" or the "harrowing of hell." "Harrowing" is an Old English word for "robbing," and "hell" is not the later Christian place of eternal punishment, but the Jewish Sheol or the Greek Hades, the afterlife place of nonexistence. Think of it as the Grave writ large. But, by either phrase, what is the meaning of that event?

To understand the full meaning of that mysterious action by Jesus on a day Mark leaves as a silent and empty Saturday, we leave the "harrowing of hell" aside for now to look first at two preliminary Jewish traditions, which will then come together to explain it when we return to it in this chapter's third section below.

GOD'S JUSTICE AND THE VINDICATION OF
THE PERSECUTED ONES

As Mark and the other evangelists set out to describe Jesus's execution, they were working within a Jewish tradition that had always emphasized how God vindicated those righteous Jews who remained faithful under persecution and were ready, if necessary, to die as martyrs for their faith in God. There were, in fact, two main models for the divine vindication of those righteous ones in the biblical tradition. And the difference concerns whether God's vindication occurred *before* or *after* their death. In other words, in one tradition God intervened to prevent their martyrdom, and in the other tradition God rewarded them after their martyrdom.

The classic example of the *first model* of divine vindication, of salvation at the last minute *before death* under persecution, is the story of Daniel in the lions' den (Dan. 5:1–6:28). In that story Daniel is depicted as a faithful Jew living among the deported leadership of his people after the destruction of the First Temple by the Babylonians at the start of the sixth century BCE. Under the last Babylonian monarch, Belshazzar, "Daniel was clothed in purple, a chain of gold was put around his neck, and a proclamation was made concerning him that he should rank third in the kingdom" (5:29). But when the Medean king Darius conquered Babylon, other high courtiers conspired against Daniel, persuaded Darius to sign a decree that for thirty days all should pray only to himself, and then accused Daniel, correctly of course, of still praying to the Jewish God three times daily.

King Darius is compelled, by his own decree but against his own will, to cast Daniel into the lions' den, but God saves Daniel:

> At break of day, the king got up and hurried to the den of lions. When he came near the den where Daniel was, he cried out anxiously to Daniel, "O Daniel, servant of the living God, has your God whom you faithfully serve been able to deliver you from the lions?" Daniel then said to the king, "O king, live forever! My God sent his angel and shut the lions' mouths so that they would not hurt me, because I was found blameless before him; and also before you, O king, I have done no wrong." (6:19–22)

Daniel is restored to his former glory, the accusers (and their families!) are devoured by the lions, and Darius commands that "in all my royal dominion people should tremble and fear before the God of Daniel" (6:26). It is the proverbial tale of all's well that ends well (except for those families!), but in a royal court setting.

No doubt that story and others like it in the biblical tradition of the just-before-death deliverance or at-the-very-last-minute salvation—think of Joseph or Susanna—would be helpful for faithful Jews facing ridicule or discrimination, but how would they help them in situations of lethal persecution when God did not intervene and they died as martyrs? That is where the second tradition became much more important.

The classic example of the *second model* of divine vindication, of salvation but only *after death*, appears in Wisdom 2–5, a book written shortly before the time of Jesus and now part of the Apocrypha of the Christian Bible. In that more generalized story, the persecutors intend to oppress the righteous ones because the latter oppose their "might makes right" philosophy and accuse them of sin:

> Let us oppress the righteous poor man; let us not spare the widow or regard the gray hairs of the aged. But let our might be our law of right, for what is weak proves itself to be useless. Let us lie in wait for the righteous man, because he is inconvenient to us and opposes our actions; he reproaches us for sins against the law, and accuses us of sins against our training. He professes to have knowledge of God, and calls himself a child of the Lord. (2:10–13)

They intend, as it were, to run a great experiment to see if God will protect the faithful:

> He calls the last end of the righteous happy, and boasts that God is his father. Let us see if his words are true, and let us test what will happen at the end of his life; for if the righteous man is God's child, he will help him, and will deliver him from the hand of his adversaries. Let us test him with insult and torture, so that we may find out how gentle he is, and make trial of his forbearance. Let us condemn him to a

shameful death, for, according to what he says, he will be protected. (2:16–20)

Next, the author continues with at least an implicit criticism of that *before-death* model, which is replaced with an *after-death* one:

But the souls of the righteous are in the hand of God, and no torment will ever touch them. In the eyes of the foolish they seemed to have died, and their departure was thought to be a disaster, and their going from us to be their destruction; but they are at peace. For though in the sight of others they were punished, their hope is full of immortality. (3:1–4)

It is, of course, that second model that is presumed behind the gospel stories of Jesus's execution and vindication. That is quite clear in Mark's account.

First, Jesus is mocked by passersby, by the authorities, and even by those crucified with him for the lack of preemptive divine intervention to save him from death on the cross, according to Mark:

Those who passed by derided him, shaking their heads and saying, "Aha! You who would destroy the temple and build it in three days, save yourself, and come down from the cross!" In the same way the chief priests, along with the scribes, were also mocking him among themselves and saying, "He saved others; he cannot save himself. Let the Messiah, the King of Israel, come down from the cross now, so that we may see and believe." Those who were crucified with him also taunted him. (15:29–32)

Second, you will recall such *future* vindication from several places in Mark's text. Apart from the three prophecies of death by execution *and* vindication by resurrection in 8:31, 9:31, and 10:33–34, the promise or threat of vindication is repeated in 13:26, "They will see 'the Son of Man coming in clouds' with great power and glory," and again in 14:62, "'You will see the Son of Man seated at the right hand of the Power,' and 'coming with the clouds of heaven.'" It is, of course, public vindication from death not before, but after it. It is not the first but the second model that is presumed behind Mark's account of Jesus's execution and all other accounts as well. Jesus's vindication was "in accordance with the scriptures" for all those who knew their tradition's second model.

GOD'S JUSTICE AND
THE BODILY RESURRECTION OF THE DEAD

Even that second model of *after-death* vindication is a very general Jewish tradition. Scholars have debated, for example, whether that divine salvation refers to the immortality of the soul or the resurrection of the body. We turn, therefore, to another and much more particular Jewish tradition, to the tradition of apocalyptic eschatology and its specification in the general bodily resurrection.

If, as in biblical tradition, your faith tells you that this world belongs to and is ruled by a just divinity and your experience tells you that the world belongs to and is ruled by an unjust humanity, *utopia* or *eschatology* becomes almost inevitable as the reconciliation of faith and experience. *Utopia*, from the Greek for "no place" or "not this place," proclaims an alternative to this present world of *place*. Eschatology, from the Greek for "about last things" or "about endings," proclaims an alternative to this present world of *time*. God, you claim, will transform this place-time world of violence and injustice into one of nonviolence and justice. God, you sing, will overcome someday. God will act, indeed must act, to make new and holy a world grown old in evil.

Eschatology is absolutely not about the end of this time-space world, but rather about the end of this time-place world's subjection to evil and impurity, injustice, violence, and oppression. It is not about the evacuation of earth for God's heaven, but about the divine transfiguration of God's earth. It is not about the destruction, but about the transfiguration of God's world here below.

As one ever more powerful empire after another took over control of Israel's fate, Jews looked more and more for God's *justification*, God's *making just* of the present world. God's Great Cosmic Cleanup became more and more fervently proclaimed and expected. An *apocalypse*, from the Greek for "revelation," is a special divine message about that eschatological event. Strictly speaking, such an apocalypse could apply to any aspect or element of eschatology, but the term *apocalyptic eschatology* usually refers to the imminence of God's transformation of this world here below from one of violent injustice to one of nonviolent justice. It never refers to the imminent end of the world as such. We, of course, can easily imagine *that* scenario because *we* can do it already in about five different ways—atomically, biologically, chemically, demographically, ecologically—and we are only up to *e*. But for ancient Jewish and Christian seers only God *could* destroy the world, but God *would* never destroy a creation judged repeatedly "good" in Genesis 1.

Granted all of that, how did the claim of general bodily resurrection, surely the most counterintuitive idea imaginable, become part of that utopian scenario of cosmic transfiguration at least within some—for example, Pharisaic—strands of Judaism? There were both a general and a specific reason. The former had to do with the transfiguration of nature, the latter with the vindication of martyrdom.

The *general* reason was because the renewal of an all-good creation here below upon this earth demanded it. How could you have a renewed creation without renewed bodies? The utopian dream of a perfect earth had three standard and intertwined components: a *physical* or pastoral world of unlabored fertility, a *feral* or animal world of vegetarian harmony, and a *social* or human world of warless peace. Here, for example, is that triple vision in *Sibylline Oracles* 3 from Egyptian Judaism between 163 and 145 BCE.

First, "The all-bearing earth will give the most excellent unlimited fruit to mortals, of grain, wine, and oil" (3:744–45). Next, "Wolves and lambs will eat grass together in the mountains" as God "will make the beasts on earth harmless" and "serpents and asps will sleep with babies and will not harm them, for the hand of God will be upon them" (3:788–95, based on Isa. 11:6–9). Finally:

> There will be no sword on earth or din of battle, and the earth will no longer be shaken, groaning deeply. There will no longer be war ... but there will be great peace throughout the whole earth.... Prophets of the great God will take away the sword for they themselves are judges of men and righteous kings. There will also be just wealth among men for this is the judgment and dominion of the great God. (3:751–55, 781–84)

That magnificent vision of a transformed earth demanded transformed flesh as well as a renewed spirit, demanded transfigured bodies as well as perfected souls.

The *specific* reason bodily resurrection became part of the utopian scenario was the problem of martyrdom during the Seleucid persecution of homeland Jews in the 160s BCE. The question was not about their survival, but about God's justice when faced specifically with the battered, tortured, and executed *bodies* of martyrs. Here the classic resurrection text is from Daniel:

> Many of those who sleep in the dust of the earth shall awake, some to everlasting life, and some to shame and everlasting contempt. Those who are wise shall shine like the brightness of the sky, and those who lead many to righteousness, like the stars forever and ever. (12:2–3)

There are even clearer texts in 2 Maccabees, where a mother and her seven sons refuse to deny God and disobey Torah even while being tortured to death. The dying words of the mother's second and third sons insist that their tortured bodies will be returned to them by God's future justice:

> And when he was at his last breath, he said, "You accursed wretch, you dismiss us from this present life, but the King of the universe will raise us up to an everlasting renewal of life, because we have died for his laws. . . . He quickly put out his tongue and courageously stretched forth his hands, and said nobly, "I got these from Heaven, and because of his laws I disdain them, and from him I hope to get them back again." (7:9–11)

Finally, "a certain Razis, one of the elders of Jerusalem" manages to outdo even the Roman Cato's noble suicidal death by falling on his sword, and "with his blood now completely drained from him, he tore out his entrails, took them in both hands and hurled them at the crowd, calling upon the Lord of life and spirit to give them back to him again" (14:37, 46). That image is biologically crude, but theologically clear. Since martyrdom is about *tortured bodies*, the justice of God requires *transfigured bodies* in the future for those disfigured bodies in the past.

Those general and specific reasons had come together in apocalyptic eschatology and Pharisaic theology at the time of Jesus. When God's Great Cleanup of the world happened—and it might well be very soon—the first order of business was the general resurrection. Since God's purpose was to establish a just and nonviolent earth, it had to start with the past before it could deal with the future. There was already a great *backlog of injustice* that had to be redeemed, a great crowd of martyrs who had to be vindicated.

If you believed, as Jesus said and Mark wrote, that the kingdom of God was already here upon the earth, you were claiming

that God's Great Cleanup had already started. And if you believed that the first act of God's Great Cleanup of the earth was
the general bodily resurrection and the vindication of all the persecuted and righteous ones, then for Christian Jews, the general
resurrection could indeed begin with Jesus, but Jesus's resurrection
would only be *along with and at the head of those other Jews who
had died unjustly or at least righteously before him.* And that is what
Jesus's "descent into hell" or "harrowing of hell" was all about—
that was what Jesus had to do on Holy Saturday. We return, finally, to those earliest Christian texts that record that magnificent
vision of divine vindication and detail what Mark did not record
about Jesus on Holy Saturday.

JESUS'S RESURRECTION AND
THE RESURRECTION OF THE RIGHTEOUS ONES

Jesus descended into hell, or Hades or Sheol, to liberate all the
righteous ones who had lived for justice and died from injustice
before he himself had lived and died a similar destiny. Jesus rose,
for those first Christian Jews, to lead God's corporate vindication
of all the righteous ones with and in himself as the supremely
Righteous One. We look at that tradition in story, hymn, image,
and finally silence.

In Story

Imagine the difficulty of fitting Jesus's harrowing of hell into a
narrative sequence on Saturday as Mark writes from Good Friday
into Easter Sunday. It is so serenely poetic and mythological that
it more or less defied the style of Mark's on-this-earth story. Even
the apparitions of the risen Jesus were all located in time and
place around Jerusalem and in Galilee and, no matter how tran-
scendentally marvelous, they could be contained within the climax of an ongoing narrative. But watch, in these two examples,

one from inside and one from outside the New Testament, how almost impossible it is to fit the harrowing of hell into that style of narrative.

The first example is Matthew 27:50–54. Watch how difficult it is for Matthew to fit a small summary of the descent-into-hell tradition as he creates his own version of Mark 15:37–39. Notice also, for future reference, that what Matthew inserts into his Markan source was already in poetic style. We place the two texts side by side so you can see easily what happens:

Mark 15:37–39	Matthew 27:50–54
³⁷Then Jesus gave a loud cry and breathed his last.	⁵⁰Then Jesus cried again with a loud voice and breathed his last.
³⁸And the curtain of the temple was torn in two, from top to bottom.	⁵¹At that moment the curtain of the temple was torn in two, from top to bottom. *The earth shook, and the rocks were split.* ⁵²*The tombs also were opened, and many bodies of the saints who had fallen asleep were raised.* ⁵³*After his resurrection they came out of the tombs and entered the holy city and appeared to many.*
³⁹Now when the centurion, who stood facing him, saw that in this way he breathed his last, he said, "Truly this man was God's Son!"	⁵⁴Now when the centurion and those with him, who were keeping watch over Jesus, saw *the earthquake and what took place, they were terrified* and said, "Truly this man was God's Son!"

Matthew inserted those two italicized sections into his Markan source—first, 27:51b–53 in between Mark 15:38 and 15:39 and then the middle of 27:54 into Mark 15:39. Why did he add those portions to Mark and what do they mean?

First, Matthew added an earthquake to the cosmic events at the death of Jesus, and that prepares for what follows. Second, there is a strange dislocation between Matthew 27:52, where the *saints were raised* on Friday evening before the resurrection of Jesus, and Matthew 27:53, where they only *appeared to many* after his resurrection. It is as if they were in a holding pattern all of Holy Saturday, but of course this is simply Matthew's attempt to fit a traditional unit about the harrowing of hell into the sequence of Mark's narrative. He is trying to both tell and not tell about Jesus's descent into hell. The saints are liberated by God's earthquake, not Jesus's presence, and they do not appear with him in resurrection, but only without him after his resurrection.

Third, Matthew uses one very significant term. He describes the resurrection of the saints "who had fallen asleep" (Greek *kekoimēmenōn*). And that is the standard way of describing the righteous ones who died before Jesus—they are not so much dead as sleeping and awaiting resurrection for their suffering and tortured or executed bodies. Two examples will suffice. Inside the New Testament, in 1 Corinthians, Paul says that "Christ has been raised from the dead, the first fruits of those who have died" (15:20). But in the Greek original, that final phrase is literally "those who were asleep" (*kekoimēmenōn*). Similarly, as we see below, outside the New Testament in the *Gospel of Peter,* the voice of God asks the rising and ascending Christ, "Have you announced [their liberation] to them that sleep [*koimōmenois*]?" and the liberated ones answered for themselves with a "yes" (42–43). We turn next to how that latter text records the harrowing of hell.

Our second example of the difficulty of fitting the harrowing of hell into a narrative style is the *Gospel of Peter* 9:35–10:42. This gospel exists only in one very tiny fragment from around 200 CE and a larger one from the 700s at the earliest. Even that larger fragment contains only the trial, execution, burial, resurrection, and apparitions, so that what we have is presumably only the end of a longer gospel. But its account of the resurrection is unique in that it actually describes the event itself as actually seen by Jewish authorities and Roman guards at the tomb. And, as you can see, it describes Jesus's resurrection at the head of "them that sleep," that is, at the head of all the persecuted righteous ones of Israel who have gone before him and now rise with him:

> In the night in which the Lord's day dawned, when the sol-
> diers, two by two in every watch, were keeping guard, there
> rang out a loud voice in heaven, and they saw the heavens
> opened and two men come down from there in a great
> brightness and draw nigh to the sepulchre. That stone
> which had been laid against the entrance to the sepulchre
> started of itself to roll and give way to the side, and the
> sepulchre was opened, and both the young men entered in.
> When now the soldiers saw this, they awakened the centu-
> rion and the elders—for they also were there to assist at the
> watch. And whilst they were relating what they had seen,
> they saw again three men come out from the sepulchre, and
> two of them sustaining the other and a cross following
> them, and the heads of the two reaching to heaven, but that
> of him who was led of them by the hand overpassing the
> heavens. And they heard a voice out of the heavens crying,
> "Have you proclaimed [liberty] to them that sleep?" and
> from the cross there was heard the answer, "Yes." (9:35–
> 10:42) *thou following*

Jesus does not ascend into heaven as in Acts 1:9, where "he was lifted up, and a cloud took him out of their sight." Instead, his body reaches from earth to heaven! And, as above with Matthew 27:50–54, we can see the difficulty of describing in a narrative the result of Jesus's harrowing of hell. It is clear enough that he has proclaimed their liberation from hell, or Sheol, to the righteous ones who have awaited his coming, have awaited him in sleep, as it were, rather than in death. But how are we to imagine that walking and talking cross? Is it a wooden cross that symbolizes their presence or do they follow Jesus in a cruciform procession? Either way, the harrowing of hell fits most uneasily into a realistic narrative sequence.

In Hymn

If the harrowing of hell fits with great difficulty into a narrative sequence, it fits with moving beauty into the poetic language of hymn and chant. Two examples will suffice.

The first is 1 Peter 3:18–19 and 4:6. 1 Peter is a circular letter written in the name of Peter toward the end of the first century, and the theme of Jesus's descent appears in a short hymn:

> For Christ also suffered for sins once for all,
> the righteous for the unrighteous,
> in order to bring you to God.
> He was put to death in the flesh,
> but made alive in the spirit,
> in which also he went and made a proclamation to the spirits
>   in prison. (3:18–19)

The proclamation is about the spirits' liberation from Hades, and this theme is repeated later in 4:6, where "the gospel was proclaimed even to the dead, so that, though they had been judged in the flesh as everyone is judged, they might live in the spirit as God does."

That preceding example is controversial as an allusion to the harrowing of hell, but there is no question about this second one. The most magnificent hymnic expression of that corporate resurrection of Jesus and the holy ones of Israel is in the *Odes of Solomon*, a collection of Christian hymns from the end of the first century. Here is its climactic celebration, in which Christ himself is the speaker:

> I was not rejected although I was considered to be so,
> and I did not perish although they thought it of me.
>
> Sheol saw me and was shattered,
> and Death ejected me and many with me.
>
> I have been vinegar and bitterness to it,
> and I went down with it as far as the depth.
>
> Then the feet and the head it released,
> because it was not able to endure my face.
>
> And I made a congregation of living among his dead;
> and I spoke with them by living lips;
> in order that my word may not fail.
>
> And those who had died ran toward me;
> and they cried out and said, "Son of God, have pity on us.
>
> And deal with us according to your kindness,
> and bring us out from the chains of darkness.
>
> And open for us the door
> by which we may go forth to you,
> for we perceive that our death does not approach you.
>
> May we also be saved with you,
> because you are our Savior."
>
> Then I heard their voice,
> and placed their faith in my heart.
>
> And I placed my name upon their head,
> because they are free and they are mine. (42:10–20)

That is a serenely poetical, metaphorical, and mythological vision in which Jesus dies and thereby descends into hell. But, since
he is the Son of God, that place cannot hold him and he bursts
asunder its locks, bolts, and bars, thereby liberating all those
whom Death and Sheol had confined before his coming. The
supremely Righteous One strides forth not alone, but at the head
of all those righteous ones who have gone before him.

In Image

It is standard in the iconography of Greek Orthodox Christianity
to depict the resurrection of Jesus not as that of an isolated individual but as that of a group in which Jesus is the liberator and
leader of the holy ones who slept in Hades awaiting his advent.
Once again two examples will suffice.

The first is St. Sargius Church in Old Cairo. The oldest part of
Cairo contains Roman, Jewish, Christian, and Muslim
buildings—an appropriate complex in which the visiting First
Lady, Hillary Rodham Clinton, urged the peoples of the Middle
East to "reject the call to violence and prejudice and discrimina-
tion" on Tuesday, March 23, 1999.

Among the Coptic Christian churches in Old Cairo is one
dedicated to Saints Sergius and Bacchus, two early fourth-
century soldier-martyrs. It was originally built in the late fourth
century and rebuilt thereafter, and its present sign announces: "St.
Sargius Church. The Oldest Church in Egypt, where the Holy
Family lived for some time during their stay in Egypt."

Be that as it may, and whether called St. Sargius, St. Sergius, or
Abu Serga, this ancient church has an exquisite set of sixteen
frescoes around its two main walls. The images detail the life of
Christ and have Arabic notations on most of them. They start
with the Annunciation, as the Holy Spirit comes upon Mary, and
end with Pentecost, as the Holy Spirit descends upon the church.
In the resurrection fresco a robed Jesus stands upon the twin

shattered gates of Hades with three figures on either side. He bends down to the left—as you face the fresco—and draws Adam and Eve from their tomb. On his other side are a bearded David and an unbearded Solomon.

The second example is the Chora Church in Istanbul. The most magnificent frescoed image of the harrowing of hell is in Istanbul's Kariye Çamii museum, once the main church of the Chora Monastery, called *chora* from its "country" location outside the fourth-century walls of Constantinople. On the southern side of the monastery is a funeral chapel whose eastern bay depicts scenes from the Last Judgment. The climactic image in the conch of the apse's ceiling is named *The Anastasis* (or "Resurrection"), but depicted is the corporate resurrection of Jesus Christ, an interpretation quite standard in Byzantine Christian iconography. First, in the center, a radiantly robed Christ reaches out with his left hand to wrench Eve and with his right hand to wrench Adam from their opened sarcophagi on either side of the fresco. For representatives of righteous ones we might have thought of better models than Adam and Eve, but Christ's saving of them indicates that many more must be imagined to be saved than can fit in that single fresco. Next, to Christ's left (viewer's right) is Abel and to his right (viewer's left) is John the Baptizer. Martyrs are, once again and always, emphasized as the center of the righteous or holy ones who await their liberation in Christ. Abel is the first martyr of the Old Testament, and John is the first martyr of the New Testament. Finally, those two martyrs lead forth the just and righteous of the Old Testament—represented by six individuals behind each of them—to heaven with Christ.

Beneath Christ's feet lies a gagged, bound, and prostrate Satan, and all around him are the broken locks and shattered doors of Hades. Christ does not rise alone but as head of all the holy ones, for how could the justice of God be established by exclusive treatment for him rather than by a community with him? Furthermore, at the entrance to the main church's inner narthex is an image of Christ Pantokrator in golden mosaic. He is named, in a superb pun, *Jesus Christ, the Chora (Country) of the Living Ones.* Exactly. Or, as Jesus said in Mark 12:27, God is "God not of the dead, but of the living."

In Silence

Jesus's harrowing of hell *may* be present in some other places in the New Testament, but those possibilities are very much debated. Indeed, it is sometimes asserted that it is a late and post–New Testament piece of theology. But there is always that version in Matthew 27:51–53, where the harrowing of hell is earlier than Matthew and included by Matthew, but is less as an example than an epitaph for the harrowing of hell tradition. It seems rather that it was early and leaving as the New Testament was being written rather than late and arriving after its creation. There are several reasons why this very early theme was steadily and almost inevitably marginalized.

First, the harrowing of hell is an intensely Jewish Christian tradition and indeed one of its most important elements, but the future did not lie with that stream of tradition.

Second, the harrowing of hell is also intensely mythological, with three linked motifs: a *deception,* in which the demons were allowed to crucify Jesus not knowing who he was; a *descent,* which was the actual reason for his death and burial; and a *despoiling,* whereby Jesus, as Son of God, broke open the prison of hell and released both himself and all the righteous ones who had preceded him there.

Third, the harrowing of hell could not fit easily into *any* sequence as the ending of a gospel narrative. How could Jesus arise at the head of the martyred and righteous ones and then appear to his disciples to give them their apostolic mandate? Such a corporate resurrection would have demanded a concomitant and immediate corporate ascension. Clearly, then, the gospel ending could have had *either* a harrowing of hell for a corporate resurrection and ascension *or* a risen apparition for apostolic commissioning, but not both. The only way to have both would have been for a corporate resurrection and ascension to have taken place *before* a return of Jesus from heaven to earth for apostolic commissioning. But that solution would create its own problems of a Jesus ascending and descending several times, and if Jesus did that, then why might he not do it afterward and always?

Fourth, there is this somewhat complicated dogmatic problem. If Christians had to be baptized in order to enter heaven, did those holy ones whom Jesus liberated from Hades enter heaven without baptism? And how could that be? After all, if baptism could be omitted for them, could it not be omitted for Christians as well?

The first and most obvious solution is that Jesus had to baptize all those holy ones in Hades before they could enter heaven with him. An example of this response is in the *Epistle of the Apostles* (*Epistula Apostolorum*), a document from the middle of the second century. Jesus himself is speaking:

> On that account I have descended and have spoken with Abraham and Isaac and Jacob, to your fathers the prophets, and have brought to them news that they may come from the rest which is below into heaven, and have given them the right hand of the baptism of life and forgiveness and pardon for all wickedness as to you, so from now on also to those who believe in me. (27)

That solves the problem quite clearly. Jesus baptized the righteous ones of the Old Testament *just as* must be done for all future believers. But then another dogmatic question could be raised. Was it appropriate that Jesus himself should do the baptizing? Maybe it was his ministers and not he himself who performed that ritual function.

That question is answered in another text from the first half of the second century called the *Shepherd of Hermas.* Its third section, the *Similitudes,* suggests that the harrowing of hell was produced not by Jesus himself, but by his apostles and teachers, who, as they died, proclaimed liberation to the holy ones and also baptized them before they entered heaven:

> These apostles and teachers, who preached the name of the Son of God, having fallen asleep in the power and faith of the Son of God, preached also to those who had fallen asleep before them and themselves gave to them the seal of the preaching. They went down therefore with them into the water and came up again, but the latter went down alive and came up alive, while the former, who had fallen asleep before, went down dead but came up alive. Through them, therefore, they were made alive and received the knowledge of the name of the Son of God. (9.16.5–7)

The Greek word translated there as "preached" is actually "proclaimed." The harrowing of hell, whether by Jesus himself or the apostles in his place, was not about preaching a sermon, but proclaiming a liberation.

For those four reasons and especially in view of dogmatic problems like that last one, the harrowing of hell tradition was necessarily lost to the gospel story, but not of course to the wider Christian tradition, especially to Christian poetry and art, hymn and image.

KINGDOM OF GOD, SON OF MAN, AND BODILY RESURRECTION

We return in conclusion to place Mark against all of that Saturday theology from outside his gospel version. We are hearing three different but equal ways of making the same claim:

1. The kingdom of God has already begun.

2. The Son of Man has already arrived.

3. The bodily resurrection has already started.

At the very start of Mark's gospel account, he had given this as his summary of Jesus's proclamation: "The time is fulfilled, and the kingdom of God has come near; repent, and believe in the good news" (1:15). That phrase "has come near" almost certainly means "is already present," but there is another theme in Mark that confirms and guarantees that interpretation. That is his vision of Jesus as the Son of Man. *For Mark the kingdom of God is already here because the Son of Man is already present.*

Recall, therefore, all that we said about Jesus as the Son of Man in Mark when discussing the trial of Jesus on Thursday in our Chapter 5. As we saw there, Mark insists that Jesus is the Son of Man from Daniel 7:13–14:

As I watched in the night visions, I saw one like a human being [literally, a son of man] coming with the clouds of heaven. And he came to the Ancient One [i.e., God] and was presented before him. To him was given dominion and glory and kingship, that all peoples, nations, and languages should serve him. His dominion is an everlasting dominion that shall not pass away, and his kingship is one that shall never be destroyed.

But the angelic interpretation of that vision in Daniel 7:27 explains that the kingdom of God is given to the Human One *for all of God's people* and not, as it were, for private privilege only:

The kingship and dominion and the greatness of the kingdoms under the whole heaven shall be given to the people of the holy ones of the Most High; their kingdom shall be

an everlasting kingdom, and all dominions shall serve and
obey them.

Actually, of course, we would already have expected that meaning and result. The beastly ones from the chaotic sea were not just
personifications, but at once emperors and the empires they
incarnated. They were corporate symbols for the Babylonian,
Medean, Persian, and Macedonian empires as well as for its
derivative Syrian empire. So also with their opposite, the Human
One, or Son of Man. He was not just a personification, but a
leader and representative of all God's people—not he without
them, not they without him.

For Mark, therefore, Jesus as Son of Man has been given the
anti-imperial kingdom of God to bring to earth for God's people,
for all those willing to enter it or take it upon themselves. Mark
insists from one end of his gospel account to the other, from 2:10
through 14:62, that Jesus as the Human One is already here below
with full authority, that he must pass through death to resurrection, and that he will (soon) return with full heavenly power and
glory. It is because Jesus as the Human One (Son of Man) from
Daniel 7 is already present on earth that the kingdom of God is
already here for all willing to pass through death to resurrection
with Jesus.

The above three claims, about the kingdom of God as already
begun through Jesus, the Son of Man as already arrived in Jesus,
and the general bodily resurrection as already started with Jesus,
intertwine with one another, serve to interpret one another, and,
taken together, reveal the heart of Mark's theology. He also insists, of course, that first, there will be a future consummation for
God's Great Cleanup, which has already started (13:26–27); second, that consummation was not supposed to happen, as some
Christian Jews had believed, at the destruction of Jerusalem (13:5–
6, 21–23); and third, consummation would be within his contemporary generation's lifetime (e.g., 9:1).

There was for Jesus, for earliest Christianity, and for Mark, one equally stunning and necessarily concomitant claim for that basic one about the *already present* kingdom of God, Son of Man, and general resurrection. If God's Great Cleanup, God's Eastertide Spring Cleaning of the world, had already begun, then it was as a collaborative effort. It was not, as it might have been imagined, an instantaneous flash of divine light, but an interactive process between divinity and humanity, a joint operation between God and ourselves. It is not us without God, or God without us. It is not that we wait for God, but that God waits for us. That is why, from one end of Mark to the other, Jesus does not travel alone, but always, always with those companions who represent us all, the named ones who fail him and the unnamed ones who do not.

———•◆•———

EIGHT

EASTER SUNDAY

When the sabbath was over, Mary Magdalene, and Mary the mother of James, and Salome bought spices, so that they might go and anoint him. And very early on the first day of the week, when the sun had risen, they went to the tomb. They had been saying to one another, "Who will roll away the stone for us from the entrance to the tomb?" When they looked up, they saw that the stone, which was very large, had already been rolled back. As they entered the tomb, they saw a young man, dressed in a white robe, sitting on the right side; and they were alarmed. But he said to them, "Do not be alarmed; you are looking for Jesus of Nazareth, who was crucified. He has been raised; he is not here. Look, there is the place they laid him. But go, tell his disciples and Peter that he is going ahead of you to Galilee; there you will see him, just as he told you." So they went out and fled from the tomb, for terror and amazement had seized them; and they said nothing to anyone, for they were afraid.

MARK 16:1–8

———•◆•———

——————— ◆ ———————

Without Easter, we wouldn't know about Jesus. If his story had ended with his crucifixion, he most likely would have been forgotten—another Jew crucified by the Roman Empire in a bloody century that witnessed thousands of such executions. Perhaps a trace or two about him would have shown up in Josephus or in Jewish rabbinic sources, but that would have been all. Indeed, without Easter, we wouldn't even have "Good Friday," for there would have been no abiding community to remember and give meaning to his death.

So Easter is utterly central. But what was it? What are the Easter stories about? On one level, the answer is obvious: God raised Jesus. Yes. And what does this mean? Is it about the most spectacular miracle there's ever been? Is it about the promise of an afterlife? Is it about God proving that Jesus was indeed his Son?

When we think about Easter, we must consider several foundational questions. What kind of stories are the Easter stories? What kind of language are they told in, and how is that language being used? Are they intended as historical reports and thus to be understood as history remembered (whether correctly or incorrectly)? Or do they use the language of parable and metaphor to express truths that are much more than factual? Or some combination of the two?

Those of us who grew up Christian have a "preunderstanding" of Easter, just as we do of Good Friday and Christmas, that shapes our hearing of these stories. So do most people who aren't Christian but who have heard something about Christianity. Usually formed in childhood, this preunderstanding is the product of combining Easter stories from all the gospels into a composite and then seeing the whole through the filter of Christian preaching and teaching, hymns and liturgy. We bring this preunderstanding of what Easter is about to the gospel stories.

This widespread preunderstanding emphasizes the historical

factuality of the stories, in harder or softer forms. The hard form, affirmed by Christians committed to biblical inerrancy, sees every detail as factually, literally, and infallibly true.[14] Many other Christians affirm a softer form. Aware of differences in the stories, they do not insist on the factual exactitude of every detail. They know that witnesses to an event can differ on details (think of diverging testimonies about an auto accident), but still be reliable witnesses to the basic factuality of the event (the accident really happened).

So the softer form does not worry about whether there was one angel (Mark and Matthew) or two (Luke) at the tomb, or about how to combine the stories that Jesus's followers experienced him in and around Jerusalem, where they stayed until Pentecost (Luke), with the story that they returned to Galilee, where they first experienced the risen Jesus (Matthew and, implicitly, Mark). But the softer form does affirm the historical factuality of "the basics": the tomb really was empty; this was because God transformed the corpse of Jesus (and not, for example, because somebody stole the body or because they went to the wrong tomb); and Jesus really did appear to his followers after his death in a form that could be seen, heard, and touched.[15]

So central is the historical factuality of the Easter stories for many Christians that, if they didn't happen this way, the foundation and truth of Christianity disappear. To underline this claim, a verse from Paul is often quoted: "If Christ has not been raised, then our proclamation has been in vain and your faith has been in vain" (1 Cor. 15:14). We agree with this statement, even as we do not think that it intrinsically points to the historical factuality of an empty tomb.[16]

But we are convinced that an emphasis on the historical factuality of the Easter stories, as if they were reporting events that could have been photographed, gets in the way of understanding them. On the one hand, it is a stumbling block for people who have difficulty believing that these stories are factual. If these think that believing these stories to be historically factual is essential to being Christian, they think they can't be Christian.[17] The issue is not simply whether "things like this" ever happen. Rather, the issue is generated by the stories themselves: their differences are difficult to reconcile, and their language often seems to be other than the language of historical reporting.[18]

Moreover, focusing on the factuality of these stories often misses their more-than-factual meanings. When treated as if they are primarily about an utterly unique spectacular event, we often do not get beyond the question, "Did they happen or not?" to the question, "What do they mean?"

HISTORY OR PARABLE?

And so we before we turn to Mark's story of Easter, we return to the foundational question with which we began. What kind of narratives are these? For instructional purposes, we pose two options—they are either history or parable. And we begin by explaining precisely what we mean by these options.

When these stories are seen as *history*, their purpose is to report publicly observable events that could have been witnessed by anybody who was there. If you or we (or Pilate) had been there when an angel rolled away the stone from the entrance to the tomb (as the guards were in Matthew's story), we would have seen it happen. If you or we (or Pilate) had gone to the tomb, we would have seen that the tomb was empty. If you or we (or Pilate) had been in the room in Jerusalem when Jesus appeared to his disciples, we would have seen him. To call these stories "history," as we are using the word here, means that the events they report could have been photographed or videotaped, if only these technologies had been available then.

When we see these stories as *parable*, the "model" for this understanding is the parables of Jesus. Christians agree that the meaning of Jesus's parables is not dependent upon whether they are historically factual. We don't know any Christians who worry about whether there really was a good Samaritan who came to the rescue of a man who had been robbed and beaten by bandits or whether there really was a father who lavishly welcomed home his prodigal son, or who would say that these stories aren't true just because they didn't happen.

The obvious insight is that parables can be true—truthful and truth-filled—independently of their factuality. Because of the importance of this insight, we state it again in only slightly different language: *the truth of a parable—of a parabolic narrative—is not dependent on its factuality.* And an additional obvious insight is that to worry or argue about the factual truth of a parable misses its point. Its point is its meaning. And "getting a parable" is getting its meaning—and often there's more than one.

Seeing the Easter stories as parable does not involve a denial of their factuality. It's quite happy leaving the question open. What it does insist upon is that *the importance of these stories lies in their meanings,* to say something that sounds almost redundant. But we risk redundancy because of the importance of the statement. To illustrate, an empty tomb without meaning ascribed to it is simply an odd, even if exceptional, event. It is only when meaning is ascribed to it that it takes on significance. This is the function of parable and parabolic language. Parable can be based on an actual event (there could have been an actual good Samaritan who did what the character in Jesus's parable is reported to have done), but it need not be.

Seeing the Easter stories as parable, as parabolic narratives, affirms, "Believe whatever you want about whether the stories happened this way—now let's talk about what they mean." If you believe the tomb was empty, fine; now, what does this story mean? If you believe that Jesus's appearances could have been videotaped, fine; now, what do these stories mean? And if you're not sure about that, or even if you are quite sure it *didn't* happen this way, fine; now, what do these stories mean?

Importantly, parable and parabolic language can make truth claims. They do not simply illustrate something as, for example, one might think of the parable of the good Samaritan as an illustration of the importance of being a neighbor to whomever is in need. Rather, as in the story of the prodigal son, they can make a truth claim: God is like the father who is overjoyed at his son's return from exile in "a far country." God is like that.

So one should not think of history as "true" and parable as "fiction" (and therefore not nearly as important). Only since the Enlightenment of the seventeenth century have many people thought this way, for in the Enlightenment Western culture began to identify truth with "factuality." Indeed, this identification is one of the central characteristics of modern Western culture. Both biblical literalists and people who reject the Bible completely do this: the former insist that the truth of the Bible depends on its literal factuality, and the latter see that the Bible cannot be literally and factually true and therefore don't think it is true at all.

But parable, independently of historical factuality, can be profoundly true. Indeed, it may be that the most important truths can be expressed only in parable. In any case, we are convinced that asking about the parabolic meaning of biblical stories, including the Easter stories, is always the most important question. The alternative of fixating on "whether it happened this way" almost always leads one astray.[19]

And so, as we turn to the stories of Easter in the New Testament, beginning with Mark, we shall highlight their meaning as parable, as truth-filled stories, without any intrinsic denial of their factuality. We are convinced that the truth claims of these stories matter most.

MARK'S STORY OF EASTER

As the first gospel, Mark has the earliest story of Easter in the New Testament (16:1–8). Of course, Paul, writing a decade and more before Mark, refers to the resurrection of Jesus, but Mark provides us with the first story, the first narrative, of Easter. For more than one reason, his story should surprise us:

- It is very brief, only eight verses. To compare the other gospels, Matthew's Easter narrative has twenty verses; Luke's, fifty-three verses; and John's, fifty-six verses divided into two chapters.

- Mark does not report an appearance of the risen Jesus. Appearance stories are found only in the other gospels.

- Mark's Easter story ends very abruptly.

As we now report how Mark tells the story of Easter, we will also note the changes that Matthew and Luke make as they incorporate Mark's text into their stories of Easter. Our purpose is not to engender skepticism, as if we were seeking to discredit witnesses by pointing out differences, but to continue reflection about the question, What kind of stories are these?

Mark's story begins with the women who saw Jesus's death and burial going to the tomb to anoint Jesus's body:

When the sabbath was over, Mary Magdalene, and Mary the mother of James, and Salome bought spices, so that they might go and anoint Jesus. And very early on the first day of the week, when the sun had risen, they went to the tomb. (16:1–2)

As they make their way there, they wonder, "Who will roll away the stone for us from the entrance to the tomb?" When they arrive, their question becomes irrelevant. "They saw that the stone, which was very large, had already been rolled back" (16:3–4).

Matthew adds two details to this portion of Mark's Easter story. First, he explains how the stone got moved: there is an earthquake, and an angel whose appearance was like lightning and whose clothing was white as snow rolls away the stone from the entrance to the tomb. Second, Matthew alone narrates the presence of guards at the tomb (27:62–66), and the appearance of the angel terrifies them so that they become "like dead men" (28:2–4). Later, Matthew tells us that the guards report what they have seen to the chief priests and elders, who bribe them to say that Jesus's disciples stole the body while they were asleep (28:11–15).

Back to Mark. The women enter the tomb, and there they see "a young man, dressed in a white robe, sitting on the right side." They are alarmed, afraid. But the young man (presumably an angel) says to them: "Do not be alarmed. You are looking for Jesus of Nazareth, who was crucified. He has been raised; he is not here. Look, there is the place they laid him" (16:5–6). Matthew makes it explicit that "the young man" is an angel (28:5). Luke adds a second figure so his story has two angels (24:4).

Mark then tells us that the women are given a commission: "But go, tell his disciples and Peter that he is going ahead of you to Galilee; there you will see him, just as he told you" (16:7). Though Mark does not report any appearances of the risen Jesus, his story does contain the promise that his disciples will see Jesus in Galilee.

Then Mark's story abruptly ends: "So the women went out and fled from the tomb, for terror and amazement had seized them; and they said nothing to anyone, for they were afraid" (16:8). The ending is not only abrupt, but puzzling. According to Mark, the women don't tell anybody. End of gospel. Full stop. The ending was deemed unsatisfactory as early as the second century, when a longer ending was added to Mark (16:9–20).[20]

In different ways, Matthew and Luke change the ending of Mark's story. Matthew reports that the women *did* tell the disciples: "They left the tomb quickly with fear and great joy, and ran to tell his disciples" (28:8). So does Luke (24:9). In addition, Luke changes the angelic commission given to the women. In Mark (and in Matthew), the women are to tell the disciples to *go to Galilee,* where they will see the risen Jesus. But in Luke, the risen Jesus appears in and around Jerusalem; Luke has no Easter stories set in Galilee. And so Luke replaces the command to go to Galilee with: "Remember how Jesus told you, *while he was still in Galilee,* that the Son of Man must be handed over to sinners, and be crucified, and on the third day rise again" (24:6–7).

MARK'S STORY AS PARABLE

As we now treat what Mark's story means as parable, we remind readers that this question does not require a denial of the story's factuality. It simply sets the factual issue aside. As a parable of the resurrection, the story of the empty tomb is powerfully evocative:

- Jesus was sealed in a tomb, but the tomb could not hold him; the stone has been rolled away.

- Jesus is not to be found in the land of the dead: "He is not here. Look, there is the place they laid him." Luke's comment on Mark's story underlines this meaning: "Why do you look for the living among the dead?" (24:5).

- Jesus has been raised. And as the angelic messenger tells the women this, he explicitly mentions the crucifixion. Jesus "who was crucified" by the authorities "has been raised" by God. The meaning is that God has said "yes" to Jesus and "no" to the powers who killed him. God has vindicated Jesus.

- His followers are promised: "You will see him."

And perhaps, as some scholars have suggested, the command to "go to Galilee" means, "Go back to where the story began, to the beginning of the gospel." And what does one hear at the beginning of Mark's gospel? It is about the *way* and the *kingdom*.

APPEARANCE STORIES IN THE OTHER GOSPELS

Mark's story of the empty tomb is expanded in the other gospels, all of which have "appearance stories," narratives in which the risen Jesus appears to his followers. These stories are the product of the experience and reflection of Jesus's followers in the days, months, years, and decades after his death. Strikingly, none is found in more than one gospel—striking because in the pre-Easter part of the gospels, the same story is often found in two or more gospels. But not so for appearance stories. Each evangelist has his own, suggesting that this is the way the story of Easter was told in the community for whom each wrote.

Matthew 28:9–20

Matthew has two stories. The first is very brief. As the women leave the tomb on their way to tell the disciples:

> Suddenly Jesus met them and said, "Greetings!" And they came to him, took hold of his feet, and worshiped him. Then Jesus said to them, "Do not be afraid; go and tell my brothers to go to Galilee; there they will see me." (28:9–10)

Matthew's second story (28:16–17) fulfills the promise of an appearance in Galilee. It happens on the "mountain" to which Jesus had told them to go. Mountains matter in Matthew. Jesus speaks the Sermon on the Mount on a mountain (of course), he is transfigured on a mountain, and now he gathers his disciples one last time on a mountain. The appearance itself is not described, but mentioned only in a subordinate clause, followed by the disciples' response of both adoration and uncertainty: "When they saw him, they worshiped him; but some doubted."

In the rest of the story, the risen Jesus speaks what has come to be known as the Great Commission:

> All authority in heaven and on earth has been given to me. Go therefore and make disciples of all nations, baptizing them in the name of the Father, and of the Son, and of the Holy Spirit, and teaching them to obey everything that I have commanded you. And remember, I am with you always, to the end of the age. (28:18–20)

Its contents are striking:

- To the risen Jesus, God has given "all authority in heaven and on earth." The implicit but obvious contrast is to the authorities who crucified him, the combination of local collaborators and imperial power. They appear to have authority, but they do not. Jesus is lord of heaven and earth; they are not.

- Jesus's followers are to make "disciples" of "all nations." Note that Matthew does not restrict "disciples" to the Twelve. Moreover, a disciple is not simply a believer, but one who follows the way of Jesus. According to Matthew, Jesus before his death restricted his mission to Israel alone; the risen Jesus now commands a mission to all nations, meaning not just Jews, but Gentiles as well.

- They are to teach them "to obey everything I have commanded you." What is required is obedience, not belief.

- "I am with you always." The words echo a theme announced in the story of Jesus's birth in Matthew, where he identifies

Jesus with "Emmanuel," which means "God is with us."
Now in Jesus's final words in Matthew, the Emmanuel
theme sounds again: "*I am with you* always, to the end of the
age." The risen Jesus is Emmanuel, God's abiding presence.

Luke 24:13–53

Like Matthew, Luke has two appearance stories, but they are
considerably longer. Both are set in Jerusalem (not Galilee),
where, according to Luke, the followers of Jesus remain; they are
still there at Pentecost fifty days later, according to Acts.[21]

The first is the Emmaus road story, the longest Easter narrative (24:13–35). Two followers of Jesus are walking from Jerusalem
to Emmaus, about seven miles away, on the day that we call
Easter. One is named Cleopas; the other is unnamed. The two are
joined by a stranger whom we as readers know to be the risen
Jesus. But they don't know this, don't recognize him. The stranger
asks them, "What are you discussing with each other?" They say
to him, "Are you the only stranger in Jerusalem who does not
know the things that have taken place there in these days?" And
so they tell him about Jesus, their hopes for him, and his crucifixion. The three walk together for some hours, and the stranger
talks to them about Moses and the prophets. But they still don't
recognize him.

As they draw near Emmaus, the stranger begins to leave. In
wonderfully evocative words, they implore him to stay: "Stay with
us, because it is almost evening and the day is now nearly over."
"Abide with us, fast falls the eventide," as the words of a well-
known hymn echo this story. So he stays. As they sit at table, the
stranger takes bread, blesses it, breaks it, and gives it to them.
Then, we are told, "Their eyes were opened and they recognized
him." Then what happens? "He vanished from their sight."

If we were to use but one story to make the case that Easter
stories are parabolic narratives, this is the one. It is difficult to

imagine that this story is speaking about events that could have been videotaped. Moreover, the story is marvelously suggestive. The risen Jesus opens up the meaning of scripture. The risen Jesus is known in the sharing of bread. The risen Jesus journeys with us, whether we know it or not. There are moments in which we do come to know him and recognize him. This story is the metaphoric condensation of several years of early Christian thought into one parabolic afternoon. Whether the story happened or not, Emmaus always happens. Emmaus happens again and again— this is its truth as parabolic narrative.

Luke's second appearance story (24:36–49) is set on the evening of the same day, so it is still Easter Sunday. Cleopas and his unnamed companion have returned from Emmaus to Jerusalem to tell "the eleven and their companions" about their experience. Then Jesus stands among them and says, "Peace be with you." They are terrified and think they're seeing a ghost. The rest of the story unfolds in three main parts.

The first part, in contrasting juxtaposition to the Emmaus story, emphasizes the "physicality" of the risen Jesus. Jesus invites them to touch him: "Touch me and see; for a ghost does not have flesh and blood as you see that I have." He also shows them the wounds in his hands and feet. Then he eats a piece of broiled fish. The point is that this is not just another ghost story. This is more than a ghost story.

The second part is commissioning and promise. Jesus commissions his followers to be his witnesses and to proclaim repentance and forgiveness to all nations. He promises them they will be "clothed with power from on high," a promise fulfilled by the coming of the Spirit at Pentecost in the first chapter of Acts.

In the third part, Jesus leads them to Bethany just east of Jerusalem, blesses them, and ascends into heaven. But in the first chapter of Acts, Luke "dates" the ascension of Jesus forty days later (Acts 1:3). Because he has Jesus ascend twice, once on the evening of Easter Sunday (in Luke's gospel) and once forty days later (in Acts), it is clear that the author is not concerned with "calendar time." In any case, in Luke, Easter has been a long and parabolic day.

John 20–21

John has four appearance stories spread over two chapters. Like Matthew, Mark, and Luke, John begins his story of Easter with the empty tomb (20:1–10), but it is told quite differently. Rather than a number of women, only one woman is mentioned, Mary Magdalene. She sees that the stone has been rolled away, but does not enter the tomb. Instead, she fetches Peter and the beloved disciple, who race to the tomb, enter it, find it empty except for the burial wrappings, and then return "to their homes."

Then John tells the first of his appearance stories (20:11–18). Mary Magdalene remains at the tomb, weeping. She looks in and sees two angels, who ask her, "Woman, why are you weeping?" She responds, "They have taken away my Lord, and I do not know where they have laid him." Neither she nor the two disciples thus far have understood the empty tomb to mean that Jesus has been raised. She turns, sees Jesus, but does not recognize him. Instead, she thinks he is the gardener and says to him, "Sir, if you have carried him away, tell me where you have laid him, and I will take him away." Jesus calls her by name, "Mary," and she recognizes him. Then Jesus speaks of his ascension: "Do not hold on to me, because I have not yet ascended to my Father. But go to my brothers and say to them, 'I am ascending to my Father and your Father, to my God and your God.'"

John's second appearance story (20:19–23) occurs on the evening of the same day in Jerusalem. The disciples, fearful of the authorities, are in a locked room. Jesus appears, says, "Peace be with you," and shows them the wounds in his hands and feet. He then bestows the Spirit upon them: "He breathed on them and said to them, 'Receive the Holy Spirit.'" In Acts, as noted earlier, the gift of the Spirit happens fifty days later at Pentecost, suggesting once again that the concern in these stories is not "calendar time."

Thomas, one of the Twelve, was not present, and when the other disciples tell him about their experience, he does not believe them. He says, "Unless I see the mark of the nails in his hands, and put my finger in the mark of the nails and my hand in his side, I will not believe" (20:24–25). This sets up John's third appearance story (20:26–29). It is a week later and the disciples are again in a shut room. Jesus appears and again says, "Peace be with you." After he invites Thomas to touch his wounds, Thomas exclaims, "My Lord and my God!" His words are, as we shall see, the classic early Christian affirmation of Easter.

Thomas has been treated quite negatively in much of Christian preaching and teaching. He is often held up as a negative role model. Indeed, while we were growing up, the only thing worse than being a "doubting Thomas" was to be a "Judas." But there is no condemnation of Thomas in the story. Thomas desires his own firsthand experience of the risen Jesus; he is unwilling to accept the secondhand testimony of others. And his desire is granted: Jesus appears to him. Unless they are inflected in an accusing way, the closing words of Jesus do not need to be read as a condemnation: "Have you believed because you have seen me? Blessed are those who have not seen and yet have come to believe." They simply affirm that those who believe without firsthand experience of the risen Jesus are also blessed.

After these three appearances, the gospel of John seems to come to an end: "Now Jesus did many other signs in the presence of his disciples, which are not written in this book. But these are written so that you may come to believe that Jesus is the Messiah, the Son of God, and that through believing you may have life in his name" (20:30–31). Indeed, the gospel may originally have ended here.

But then another chapter begins, reporting John's fourth appearance story (21:1–23). The first three happened in Jerusalem;

this one is set in Galilee on the shore of the Sea of Tiberias (another name for the Sea of Galilee). Seven disciples are there, and they have been fishing all night, but have caught nothing. From the shore, Jesus calls to them, though they do not know it is Jesus, and he tells them to cast their net on the other side of the boat. They do, and the net becomes so full of fish they cannot haul it in. Then the beloved disciple tells Peter, "It is the Lord," and Peter jumps into the sea, presumably to make his way to land ahead of the others.

When they get ashore, Jesus has made them a breakfast of bread and fish. After breakfast, a dialogue occurs between Jesus and Peter. Three times Jesus asks Peter, "Simon, son of John, do you love me?" Three times Peter responds, "Yes Lord, you know that I love you." Three times Jesus responds to Peter's response: "Feed my lambs," "Tend my sheep," "Feed my sheep."

Then, in figurative language, Jesus warns Peter that he will be martyred, crucified like Jesus. The dialogue concludes with, "Follow me," repeated twice (21:19, 22). Follow me on the path I have followed. They are the last words of Jesus in John's gospel.[22]

THE GOSPEL EASTER STORIES TOGETHER

Two themes run through these stories that sum up the central meanings of Easter. The first, in a concise phrase, is *Jesus lives.* He continues to be experienced after his death, though in a radically new way. He is no longer a figure of flesh and blood, confined to time and space, but a reality who can enter locked rooms, journey with followers without being recognized, be experienced in both Galilee and Jerusalem, vanish in the moment of recognition, and abide with his followers always, "to the end of the age."

Together, the appearance stories in the gospels make explicit what is promised in Mark: "You will see him." They underline the parabolic meaning of Mark's story of the empty tomb: Jesus is not among the dead, but among the living. Indeed, this is one of the central affirmations of Easter: Jesus lives. He is a figure of the present, not simply of the past. The presence his followers had known in Jesus before his crucifixion continued to be experienced and to operate after it.

As we understand this affirmation, it is not simply a statement about a brief series of experiences that occurred two thousand years ago for a period of forty days between resurrection and ascension. Luke, in his second volume, Acts, is the only New Testament author to suggest this, and it has become part of the Christian liturgical year. But, as mentioned earlier, it is clear that Luke is not writing about "calendar time": he has Jesus ascend twice, once on Easter day and again forty days later.

Rather, the truth of the affirmation "Jesus lives" is grounded in the experience of Christians throughout the centuries. Not all Christians have had such an experience. It is not essential. To quote from one of John's Easter stories, "Blessed are those who have not seen and yet believe." But some Christians to the present day have experienced Jesus as a living reality. For us, this is the experiential ground of the first of the central Easter affirmations: Jesus continues to be and to operate. The spirit, the presence, his followers knew in him before his death continues to be known. Jesus lives.

To state the second affirmation of the Easter stories in an equally concise phrase: *God has vindicated Jesus.* God has said "yes" to Jesus and "no" to the powers who executed him. Easter is not about an afterlife or about happy endings. Easter is God's "yes" to Jesus *against* the powers who killed him. The stories underline this in different ways. In Luke and John, the risen Jesus continues to bear the wounds of the empire that executed him. In Matthew, the risen Jesus has been given authority over all the authorities of this world. Mark, writing most concisely among the authors of the gospels, says simply, "You are looking for Jesus of Nazareth, *who was crucified; he has been raised.*"

The authors of the gospels do not speak about Jesus's resurrection without speaking about his crucifixion by the collusion between collaborators and imperial power. In the words of the earliest and most widespread post-Easter affirmation about Jesus in the New Testament, *Jesus is Lord.* And if Jesus is Lord, the lords of this world are not. Easter affirms that the domination systems of this world are not of God and that they do not have the final word.

PAUL AND THE RESURRECTION OF JESUS

There is one more voice to consider, Paul. As the earliest voice in the New Testament, Paul provides us with the earliest testimony to the resurrection of Jesus. The central themes of the gospel stories—*Jesus lives* and *Jesus is Lord*—are equally central to Paul's experience, conviction, and theology. To these, he adds a third. But before we consider the third, we treat the first two.

With regard to the theme *Jesus lives,* Paul experienced the risen Jesus. Writing in the 50s, Paul says in his first letter to Christians in the city of Corinth in Greece, "I have seen the Lord" (9.1).[23] Later in the same letter, after he provides a list of people to whom the risen Jesus appeared, he says, "Last of all, as to one untimely born, he appeared also to me" (15:8). In another letter, he writes, "God revealed his son to me" and that he received his gospel "through a revelation of Jesus Christ" (Gal. 1:16, 12). Another such experience may be described in 2 Corinthians 12:2–4.

But when and how did Paul experience the risen Jesus? It happened at least a few years after what we call Easter Sunday, his famous Damascus road experience. As described three times in the book of Acts, Paul saw a great light and heard the voice of Jesus (Acts 9; 22; 26; the details differ somewhat in each account). Those traveling with Paul did not share the experience, indicating that it was a private and not a public experience. In short, it was what is commonly called a vision.

It is possible, perhaps even likely, that Paul thought of the appearances of the risen Jesus to Jesus's other followers also as visions. In the list of appearances in 1 Corinthians, he uses the same verb, "appeared," for their experience and for his own:

> He [Jesus] *appeared* to Cephas [the Aramaic name of Peter], then to the twelve. Then he *appeared* to more than five hundred brothers and sisters at one time, most of whom are still alive, though some have died. Then he *appeared* to James [the brother of Jesus], then to all the apostles [for Paul, a group larger than the Twelve]. Last of all, as to one untimely born, he *appeared* also to me. (15:5–8)

Moreover, the fact that he includes his experience in this list suggests that he saw it to be like theirs.[24]

Thus Paul provides reason to think of the Easter appearance stories in the gospels as visionary in nature. Some Christians are uncomfortable with this thought, as if these were "only" visions. A reason for this notion is that we in modern Western culture tend not to think very highly of visions. We typically see them as hallucinations, as mental disturbances that have nothing to do with the way things are, as far less important than "real" seeing.

Thus it is important to emphasize that not all visions are hallucinations. They can be disclosures of reality. Moreover, visions can involve not only seeing (apparition) and hearing (audition), but even a tactile dimension, as dreams sometimes do. Thus a story in which Jesus invites his followers to touch him or is seen to eat does not intrinsically point away from a vision. People who have had a vision report that something important and meaningful, often life-changing, has happened to them—they would never consider trivializing it as "*only* a vision."

Paul came to believe *Jesus is Lord* (the second theme), because his experience of the risen Jesus changed his life. Prior to his experience on the Damascus road, he was Saul the Pharisee, a zealous persecutor of the movement that had come into existence around Jesus (Phil. 3:4–6). His experience had a crucial corollary.

It generated the conviction not only that "Jesus lives," but that God had vindicated Jesus, said "yes" to the one who had been executed by the authorities and whose movement Paul was persecuting.

In short, to use Paul's most concise affirmation, his experience of the risen Jesus led him to the conviction, "Jesus is Lord." The conviction sounds throughout his letters. And it put him on a collision course not only with the leaders of his own people, but also with imperial authority. To say "Jesus is Lord" meant "Caesar is not Lord." Imperial power crucified "the Lord of glory" (1 Cor. 2:8), but God raised him and bestowed upon him the name that is above every name. In the words of an early Christian hymn (found in full in Phil. 2:6–11), possibly written by Paul and in any case used approvingly by Paul:

> Therefore God highly exalted him and gave him the name that is above every name, so that at the name of Jesus every knee should bend, in heaven and on earth and under the earth, and every tongue should confess that Jesus Christ is Lord to the glory of God the Father. (Phil. 2:9–11)

Paul's third Easter theme makes explicit what is implicit in the gospel stories of Easter. Namely, within the world of Jewish thought that shaped Jesus, Paul, and the authors of the New Testament, resurrection was associated with eschatology. Recall, therefore, everything we said, especially in Chapter 7, about eschatology as the fervent hope for God's Great Cleanup of an unjust and violent world, about apocalyptic eschatology as the revealed imminence of that cosmic transformation, and about the bodily resurrection of the dead and the vindication of the martyrs (and of all those who had lived for justice and died from injustice), which would be the first order of divine business on that great day.

But, then, since Jesus, Paul, and earliest Christianity claimed that *God's transfiguration of this earth had already started,* they also claimed that *the general resurrection had begun with Jesus.* That, of course, is why Paul must argue in 1 Corinthians that if there is no general resurrection, there is no Jesus resurrection, and if there is no Jesus resurrection, there is no general resurrection (15:12–16). They stand or fall together. That is why he can call Jesus's resurrection "the firstfruits," or start, of the general resurrection (15:20).

If, therefore, the kingdom of God has begun on this earth or the general bodily resurrection has begun on this earth, the claim is also being made that all are here and now called to participate in what is now a collaborative eschatology. Or, in the magnificent aphorism of St. Augustine: "We without God cannot, and God without us will not."

EASTER AND CHRISTIAN LIFE TODAY: PERSONAL AND POLITICAL TRANSFORMATION

Easter completes the archetypal pattern at the center of the Christian life: death and resurrection, crucifixion and vindication. Both parts of the pattern are essential: death *and* resurrection, crucifixion *and* vindication. When one is emphasized over the other, distortion is the result. The two must be affirmed equally.

Without an emphasis on Easter as God's decisive reversal of the authorities' verdict on Jesus, the cross is simply pain, agony, and horror. It leads to a horrific theology: God's judgment means that we all deserve to suffer like this, but Jesus died in our place. God can spare us because Jesus is the substitutionary sacrifice for our sins.

Without God's reversal at Easter, Good Friday also leads to a cynical politics. This is the way the world is, the powers are and always will be in control, and those who think it can be otherwise are utopian dreamers. Christianity is about the *next* world, not this one, and this one belongs to the wealthy and powerful, world without end.

Easter without Good Friday risks sentimentality and vacuity. It becomes an affirmation that spring follows winter, life follows death, flowers will bloom again, and it is time for bonnets and bunnies. But Easter as the reversal of Good Friday means God's vindication of Jesus's passion for the kingdom of God, for God's justice, and God's "no" to the powers who killed him, powers still very much active in our world. Easter is about God even as it is about Jesus. Easter discloses the character of God. Easter means God's Great Cleanup of the world has begun—but it will not happen without us.

The archetypal pattern produced by Good Friday and Easter is both personal and political. As the climax of Holy Week and the story of Jesus, Good Friday and Easter address the fundamental human question, What ails us? Most of us feel the force of this question—something is not right. So what ails us? Very compactly, egoism and injustice. And the two go together. We need personal transformation and political transformation.

Egoism is not a biblical word, but it names a central theme of Christian thought about the human condition, shaped by a reading of the Bible and reflection about human experience. Egoism means being centered in the self and its anxieties and preoccupations, what is sometimes called the "small self." Egoism is centering in the anxious and fearful self and its concerns and desires. Alternatively, it is centering in the accomplished self, the successful self, and its achievements. Importantly, the problem is not that being a self is bad, as if the solution is ceasing to be a self. Rather, the issue is the kind of self that I am, that you are, that we are.

Good Friday and Easter, death and resurrection together, are a central image in the New Testament for the path to a transformed self. The path involves dying to an old way of being and being reborn into a new way of being. Good Friday and Easter are about this path, the path of dying and rising, of being born again.

All of the major witnesses of the New Testament testify to this. It is the "way" that Mark speaks about with his correlation of following Jesus and the path of death and resurrection. After Jesus speaks for the first time about his impending death and resurrection, he says, "If any want to become my followers, let them deny themselves and take up their cross and follow me" (8:34), thus pointing to participation in his path. Matthew and Luke take this over from Mark, and Luke adds the word "daily" (9:23) to make sure we get the point.

It is the path of transformation that Paul had experienced when he wrote, "I have been crucified with Christ; it is no longer I who live, but it is Christ who lives in me" (Gal. 2:19–20). He affirms this path for all Christians when he writes about baptism as a ritual enactment of dying and rising, death and resurrection (Rom. 6:1–11). The result is a new self, a new creation: "If anyone is in Christ, there is a new creation" (2 Cor. 5:17).

And it is the "way" at the center of John's gospel. The Jesus of John's gospel speaks explicitly about being "born again" (3:1–10). In another passage, he says that unless a grain of wheat falls into the earth and dies, it cannot bear fruit (12:24). He speaks of this way as "the only way" (14:6) in a verse that has unfortunately often become a triumphalist claim justifying Christian exclusivism. But within John's incarnational theology, the death and resurrection of Jesus incarnates the way of transformation. This is what it means to say, "Jesus is the only way." The path we see in him—dying and rising—is the path of personal transformation.[25]

So there is powerful personal meaning to Lent, Holy Week, Good Friday, and Easter. We are invited into the journey that leads through death to resurrection and rebirth. But when only the personal meaning is emphasized, we betray the passion for which Jesus was willing to risk his life. That passion was the kingdom of God, and it led him to Jerusalem as the place of confrontation with the domination system of his time, execution, and vindication. The political meaning of Good Friday and Easter sees the human problem as injustice, and the solution as God's justice.

We Christians have most often overlooked the political meaning of Holy Week. The New Testament and Jesus do not simply speak of dying, but crucifixion. Suppose Jesus had jumped off a high building to illustrate that the path of transformation is dying. To say the obvious, this would have involved a death. But the way of Jesus involves not just any kind of death, but "taking up the cross" and following him to Jerusalem, the place not only of dying and rising, but specifically of confrontation with the authorities and vindication by God.

Seeing the political meaning of Good Friday and Easter can help us to recover the political meaning of Jesus and the Bible as a whole, a meaning muted in much of Christian preaching and teaching. Barbara Ehrenreich, in her best-selling book about the working class in the United States, provides a striking example. She goes to a revival meeting attended primarily by poor people at which the preacher emphasizes going to heaven by believing in the substitutionary atonement of Jesus. She comments:

> It would be nice if someone would read this sad-eyed crowd the Sermon on the Mount, accompanied by a rousing commentary on income inequality and the need for a hike in the minimum wage. But Jesus makes his appearance here only as a corpse; the living man, the wine-guzzling vagrant and precocious socialist, is never once mentioned, nor anything he ever had to say. Christ crucified rules, and it may be that the true business of modern Christianity is to crucify him again and again so that he can never get a word out of his mouth.

She concludes: "I get up to leave, timing my exit for when the preacher's metronomic head movements have him looking the other way, and walk out to search for my car, half expecting to find Jesus out there is the dark, gagged and tethered to a tent pole."[26]

The story of Holy Week as Mark and the other gospels tell it enables us to hear the passion of Jesus—what he was passionate about—that led to his execution. His passion was the kingdom of God, what life would be like on earth if God were king, and the rulers, domination systems, and empires of this world were not. It is the world that the prophets dreamed of—a world of distributive justice in which everybody has enough and systems are fair. And it is not simply a political dream. It is God's dream, a dream that can only be realized by being grounded ever more deeply in the reality of God, whose heart is justice. Jesus's passion got him killed. But God has vindicated Jesus. This is the political meaning of Good Friday and Easter.

There is thus a strong anti-imperial theology in the gospels. Anti-imperial theology continues in Paul's affirmation that Jesus is Lord and therefore empire and the emperor are not. It resounds again in the strange book of Revelation, whose central contrast is between the lordship of Christ and the lordship of empire. Empire is the beast from the abyss, the great harlot drunk with the blood of the saints, the monster whose number is 666.[27]

The anti-imperial meaning of Good Friday and Easter is particularly important and challenging for American Christians in our time, among whom we number ourselves. The United States is the world's dominant imperial power. As we reflect about this, it is important to realize that empire is not intrinsically about geographical expansion. As a country, we may not be interested in that. But empire is about the use of military and economic power to shape the world in one's perceived interest. Within this definition, we are the Roman Empire of our time, both in our foreign policy and in the shape of economic globalization that we as a country vigorously advocate.

Christians in the United States are deeply divided about this country's imperial role. Our perception of the church in America, using very approximate estimates, is that about 20 percent of Christians are very critical of American imperial policy and about 20 percent are strong supporters of it. These supporters include, of course, our president, whose speeches identify the American way of life as "the light that shines in the darkness," words that John 1:5 applies to Jesus, who was crucified by empire. The middle of the Christian spectrum (perhaps as many as 60 percent) is undecided. Of course, they are not completely undecided; some of them lean one way or the other. Their indecision comes from a variety of causes. Some see Christianity as essentially nonpolitical and therefore do not connect their devotion to Jesus with political matters. Some, as others in our population, do not pay much attention to politics. And some find it difficult to imagine that our country is like the imperial power that crucified Jesus.

The 20 percent on the two ends of the spectrum are already deeply committed to two very different visions of Christian faithfulness. And the middle 40–60 percent is crucial for the future of the United States and the church in this country. They—perhaps you—are undecided, and thus open to seeing the full meaning of Holy Week, Good Friday, and Easter, indeed, the full story of Jesus and the Bible.

Just as there is a dangerous distortion when only the personal meaning of Good Friday and Easter is emphasized, so also when only the political meaning is emphasized. When this happens, we forget that Jesus's passion was not just the *kingdom* of God. It was also the kingdom of *God*. They go together: it is never kingdom without God, and it is never God without kingdom. It is a deeply religious vision of life under the lordship of God as known in Jesus, which is the same as life under the lordship of Christ.

"Jesus is Lord," the most widespread post-Easter affirmation in the New Testament, is thus both personal and political. It involves a deep centering in God, a deep centering in God that includes radical trust in God, the same trust that we see in Jesus. It produces freedom—"For freedom, Christ has set us free"; compassion—the greatest of the spiritual gifts is love; and courage—"Fear not, do not be afraid." Without this personal centering in God, Dietrich Bonhoeffer would not have had the freedom and courage to engage in a conspiracy against Hitler within Nazi Germany itself. Without it, Desmond Tutu could not have opposed apartheid with such courage, infectious joy, and a reconciling spirit. Without it, Martin Luther King, Jr., could not have kept on keeping on in the midst of all the threats that he faced.

And this deep centering also involves loyalty, allegiance, and commitment to God as disclosed in Jesus. Such loyalty is the opposite of idolatry, of giving one's loyalty to a lesser good. It also involves loyalty and commitment to God's passion as disclosed in Jesus, a passion for compassion, justice, and nonviolence. Compassion—love—is utterly central to the message and life of Jesus, and justice is the social form of compassion. To put the same thought in different language, love is the soul of justice, and justice is the body, the flesh, of love.

All of this is what Easter, the ultimate climax of Holy Week, is about. Good Friday, the penultimate climax, discloses how powerful the forces arrayed against the kingdom of God are. Easter affirms, "Jesus is Lord"—the powers of this world are not. Holy Week, Good Friday, and Easter are about the conflict between the radicality of God and the normalcy of domination systems, which is the normalcy of civilization. Jesus's last week challenges the domination systems of this world even as it also invites us upon a journey through death to resurrection, journeying with the risen Jesus, the risen Christ.

The personal and political meanings of Holy Week are captured in two nearly identical questions. The first is one that many Christians have heard and responded to: Do you accept Jesus as your personal Lord and Savior? It is a crucially important question, for the Lordship of Christ is the path of personal liberation, return from exile, and conscious reconnection to God. The virtually identical but seldom asked question is: Do you accept Jesus as your political Lord and Savior? The gospel *of* Jesus, the good news *of* Jesus, which is the gospel of the kingdom of God, involves both questions. The gospel *about* Jesus, the good news *about* Jesus, which is the gospel of the Lordship of Christ, involves both questions.

Holy Week and the journey of Lent are about an alternative procession and an alternative journey. The alternative procession is what we see on Palm Sunday, an anti-imperial and nonviolent procession. Now as then, that procession leads to a capital city, an imperial center, and a place of collaboration between religion and violence. Now as then, the alternative journey is the path of personal transformation that leads to journeying with the risen Jesus, just as it did for his followers on the road to Emmaus. Holy Week as the annual remembrance of Jesus's last week presents us with the always relevant questions: Which journey are we on? Which procession are we in?

NOTES

---·◆·---

1. George Caird, professor of New Testament at Oxford and author of many books.

2. In a minor way that produces an almost comic result, the author of Matthew misunderstands the passage from Zechariah (perhaps because he was using the Greek version of the Hebrew Bible, the Septuagint). Namely, he reads the passage as if it refers to two animals: a donkey *and* a colt, the foal of a donkey. So Matthew adds a second animal to the story. Thus, in Matthew, Jesus enters Jerusalem riding on two animals, not one, and presumably of different sizes. One cannot really imagine it. But the author of Matthew correctly recognizes that the story in Mark is based on the passage from Zechariah.

3. Here, as elsewhere, "the nations" are the gentile nations, especially the gentile empires that had ruled over the Jewish people.

4. See Walter Brueggemann, the foremost Hebrew Bible scholar in the United States today, *The Prophetic Imagination* (Philadelphia: Fortress, 1978), Chapter 2.

5. The fact that this oracle is found in two different prophets suggests that it was a common hope in prophetic circles.

6. For a description of Herod's palace, see Ann Wroe, *Pontius Pilate* (New York: Random House, 1999), pp. 76–77.

7. For a persuasive argument that this was happening with increasing frequency in the first century, see Martin Goodman, *The Ruling Class of Judaea* (Cambridge: Cambridge University Press, 1987), pp. 55–58.

8. Daryl Schmidt, *The Gospel of Mark* (Sonoma, CA: Polebridge, 1990), pp. 3–6.

9. Matthew changes Mark's report of Jesus's response into a resounding affirmation: "Blessed are you, Simon, son of Jonah! For flesh and blood has not revealed this to you, but my Father in heaven" (16:17).

10. Matthew loses this point in his rephrasing of Mark by dropping the reference to *two disciples* and reporting that Jesus sent *the disciples* (presumably including Judas) to make the arrangements (Matt. 26:17–19).

11. For fuller but still concise expositions, see Marcus Borg (with N. T. Wright), *The Meaning of Jesus: Two Visions* (San Francisco: HarperSanFrancisco, 1999), pp. 137–42; and Marcus Borg, *The Heart of Christianity* (San Francisco: HarperSanFrancisco, 2003), pp. 91–96.

12. See also Marcus Borg, *Reading the Bible Again for the First Time* (San Francisco: HarperSanFrancisco, 2001), pp.256–57.

13. For this suggestion, see Ched Myers, *Binding the Strong Man* (Maryknoll, NY: Orbis, 1988), p. 378, a superb political reading of Mark's gospel.

14. We note in passing that there is no intrinsic connection between "infallibility" and "inerrancy" and reading the Bible literally and factually. There is no reason why God could not speak infallibly in the language of poetry and parable, song and symbol, metaphor and myth. But in the modern period, "biblical infallibility" and literal-factual interpretation generally accompany each other.

15. A number of additional emphases usually go with an emphasis upon the historical factuality of the Easter stories (in harder or softer form). First, Easter is utterly unique; this is the one and only time that something like this has happened. Second, its spectacular uniqueness demonstrates that Jesus really is the Son of God and that Christianity is true. Finally, Easter is commonly connected to our hope for an afterlife: at Easter, God demonstrated that death is not the end.

16. Paul's point is that if God has not said "yes" to Jesus, if God has not vindicated Jesus, then our faith is in vain. But, as we shall see, Paul does not emphasize an empty tomb. Rather, he grounds his confidence in Jesus's resurrection in the appearances of Jesus to his followers and ultimately to Paul himself, which Paul understands as visions.

17. We note in passing that probably more people have left the church because of biblical literalism than for any other reasons. Though we are not aware of any polls about this, it fits our experience of people who have left the church.

18. There are at least two additional difficulties with a literal-factual reading of the Easter stories. The first is that it requires a "supernatural interventionist" understanding of the way God relates to the world. Minimally, it requires that we think of the stones being rolled away by God or an angel (and in either case, by supernatural agency), and that

we think of God transforming the corpse of Jesus so that it was no longer in the tomb. But does God ever act this way? Is this an illuminating way to think of the way God acts in the world? The second difficulty is that a literal-factual reading of these texts most commonly emphasizes that Easter is utterly unique, that God has not done this kind of thing anywhere or anytime else, and thus it privileges Christianity as the only true or "full" revelation of God, the "only way."

19. A classic example in both church and culture today is thinking that the truth of the Genesis stories of creation depends upon their factuality. This has led to disputes about "creation" versus "evolution," "intelligent design" versus "random evolution," and so forth. These disputes would not have occurred without the modern (Enlightenment) conviction that truth equals factuality. For many defenders of the "truth of Genesis," the truth of these stories is dependent upon their factuality, and evolution is a competing factuality. A parabolic reading of these stories would eliminate this conflict and place the issue where it really belongs: To whom does the earth belong? Is it the creation of God and the gift of God, wondrous and calling forth awe, plenteous and calling forth gratitude and adoration, and intended for the whole of creation? Or is it ours?

20. Some scholars argue that Mark's gospel likely did not end with verse 8, perhaps because Mark did not have a chance to finish it or perhaps because the ending got separated from the rest of the manuscript. But most scholars affirm that 16:8 is the original ending.

21. Indeed, according to Luke, Jesus tells them to stay in the city (24:49) and they do so (24:52–53). At the beginning of Acts, written by the author of Luke, they are still there in obedience to the command (Acts 1:4).

22. The first words of Jesus in John's gospel are, "What are you looking for?" (1:38); in the middle of the gospel, Jesus says, "I am the way" (14:6); and at the end, Jesus says, "Follow me" (twice, 21:19, 22).

23. In the same verse, he asks rhetorically, "Am I not free? Am I not an apostle?" Paul links freedom to an experience of the risen Jesus, even as he also links apostleship to such an experience. We note that for Paul, the "apostles" are a larger group than the Twelve and include women. See Romans 16.7, where a woman named Junia is said to be "prominent among the apostles."

24. Though there is some overlap between Paul's list and the gospel stories, the correlation is not precise. Paul does not mention appearances

to women, and the gospels do not mention appearances to James the brother of Jesus or to five hundred people at one time (though some have wondered if this could be the Pentecost experience narrated in Acts 2).

25. For a fuller treatment of the path of personal transformation, see Marcus Borg, *The Heart of Christianity* (San Francisco: HarperSanFrancisco, 2003), pp. 103–25.

26. Barbara Ehrenreich, *Nickel and Dimed* (New York: Henry Holt, 2001), pp. 68–69.

27. For these claims, see any mainstream scholarly commentary on Revelation. For a concise chapter-length treatment, see Marcus Borg, *Reading the Bible Again for the First Time* (San Francisco: HarperSanFrancisco, 2001), pp. 265–96.